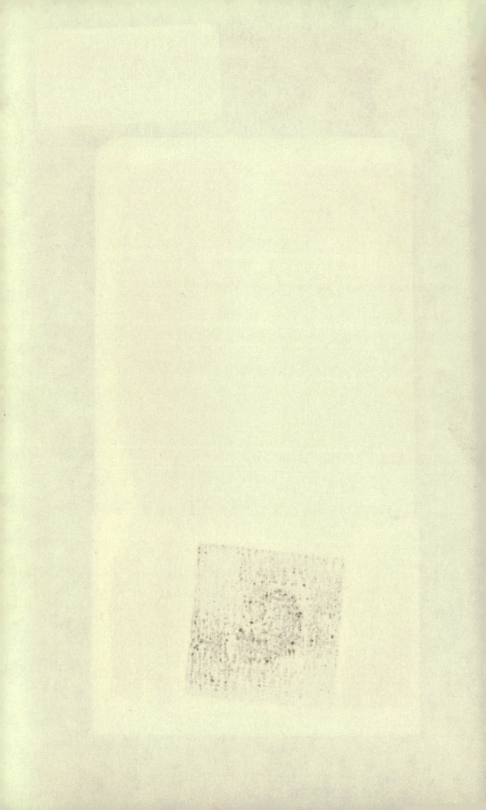

THE
SUNDANCE
KID

THE
SUNDANCE
KID

The Life of Harry Alonzo Longabaugh

Donna B. Ernst

Foreword by Daniel Buck and Anne Meadows
Introduction by Paul D. Ernst

UNIVERSITY OF OKLAHOMA PRESS : NORMAN

This book is published with the generous assistance of The Kerr Foundation, Inc.

Library of Congress Cataloging-in-Publication-Data

Ernst, Donna B., 1946–
    The Sundance Kid : the life of Harry Alonzo Longabaugh / Donna B. Ernst ; foreword by Daniel Buck and Anne Meadows ; introduction by Paul D. Ernst.
        p.   cm.
    Includes bibliographical references and index.
    ISBN 978-0-8061-3982-1 (hardcover : alk. paper)
    1. Sundance Kid. 2. Outlaws—West (U.S.)—Biography. 3. Ranch life—West (U.S.)—History—19th century. 4. Bank robberies—West (U.S.)—History—19th century. 5. Train robberies—West (U.S.)—History—19th century. 6. West (U.S.)—Biography. 7. Outlaws—South America—Biography. I. Title.
    F595.S94E755 2009
    978'.02092—dc22
    [B]
                                                                    2008021826

The paper in this book meets the guidelines for permanence and durability of the Committee on Production Guidelines for Book Longevity of the Council on Library Resources, Inc. ∞

1 2 3 4 5 6 7 8 9 10

For Paul, Daniel, Autumn, and Cassidy

Contents

Illustrations

Unless otherwise credited, photographs are from the author's collection.

Foreword

Daniel Buck and Anne Meadows

Butch and Sundance will forever roll off the tongue as a single word, thanks to the movie *Butch Cassidy and the Sundance Kid.* If not quite so entwined early in life, the pair did escape down to Argentina together (Sundance had the foresight to bring along a female companion), and some years later they died side by side. Thus Butch and Sundance are tattooed in our mind, like Frank and Jesse, Bonnie and Clyde, not to mention Lewis and Clark, Grant and Lee, Abbott and Costello, and a host of other American geminates.

Sundance's expatriation to the Southern Hemisphere was not without reason. If a wanted man desires a new life, it helps to change theaters. He tried to do just that by immigrating to Argentina, a land in 1901 as full of promise as the American West once was to the teenage Harry Longabaugh (not yet Sundance) slipping out from Pennsylvania. But his past was never far behind him, and after an idyllic period ranching in Patagonia, he and his colleagues were on the run again.

Sundance left no diary, and only a couple of his letters have survived. One was published in a Wyoming newspaper that had compared his escapades to those of Jesse James. At that point he was but a twenty-year-old cowboy accused of stealing a horse. He complained that the article was "very sensational and partly untrue." Had Jesse James been in a position to post his own letter—he was not, having been killed some years earlier—he might have griped about being aligned with a callow horse thief. No matter. Within a few years Sundance had graduated to an assaulter of banks and a robber of trains. The sensational approximated the true.

Newspapers ballyhoo outlaws' exploits—often spun out of wisps of rumor—that their own families hush up. Bandits themselves perforce lead secret lives. What scarce outlaw memoirs exist were leaked from the pens of the few who retired and went straight, who lived into old age. Sundance was forty-one when he died in Bolivia; too old to change his ways but too young to write his memoirs.

Fortunately for us, Donna Ernst took up the challenge. *The Sundance Kid: The Life of Harry Alonzo Longabaugh* is the story of an illustrious—if at times delinquent—Longabaugh ancestor, assiduously researched and engagingly told.

Introduction

Paul D. Ernst

As you enter the public library in Phoenixville, Pennsylvania, near where I live, your attention is drawn to two exhibits across from one another. They display the lives of two well-known native sons—Samuel Pennypacker, one of Pennsylvania's early governors, and Harry A. Longabaugh, my great-great uncle, better known as the Sundance Kid. Most people might say the governor was the more important citizen, and I agree. But being related to an outlaw has been a lot more fun and exciting.

Beginning in the 1770s, two brothers named Baltzer and Conrad traveled separately from Germany to the Colonies just in time to participate in the Revolutionary War. Neither brother could read nor write, and upon arrival—Baltzer in Baltimore and Conrad in Philadelphia—their surname was apparently spelled phonetically by immigration authorities, ship captains, and eventually enlistment officers. They became Baltzer Langenbaugh and Conrad Longabaugh. Today there are about a dozen spellings of the original name, but our immediate lineage has always and only used two variations— Longabaugh and Longabough.

Although they continued to live miles apart, the brothers remained in touch with each other. Baltzer's line tended to move frequently, but Conrad's family has lived in the Phoenixville, Chester County, area since his arrival in 1772. Across the Schuylkill River and Canal from Phoenixville is the quaint village of Mont Clare, Montgomery County, where Sundance was born and raised. The two towns are located thirty miles from Philadelphia on the canal and railroad line. Steel production, agriculture, and transportation were the main industries that gave the region its start. Within five miles are the fields and meadows of Valley Forge, where Washington and his men trained and regrouped during the harsh winter of 1777 and 1778.

Today many of the houses, schools, and buildings that Sundance would have known before he left in 1882 still exist. Each June, the communities of Phoenixville and Mont Clare celebrate "Canal Days" in commemoration of their joint history. The canal and river are still used for small boating, but the large canal barges filled with coal that were pulled by mules from upstate are long gone.

In this conservative and devoutly religious place, Sundance would have had a family-oriented upbringing. With two sisters and two brothers, money was definitely a problem; so he worked for farmers and attended school between harvesting and planting. The family usually rented the farm where his father, Josiah, worked. Living on a canal with barges going by continually to Philadelphia probably gave Sundance a yearning to explore the country. His oldest brother, Elwood, left home approximately the same time that Sundance left to become a whaler, eventually settling in San Francisco.

As a child, I wasn't aware of my connection to the Sundance Kid. Sometimes a comment was made by my grandfather, William H. Longabough, to his son Bill in reference to having a wayward relative; but then Grandpop would just smile and change the subject when asked for details. In his final weeks of life, Grandpop developed dementia, probably from his medication. He died in March of 1976 without sharing anything he knew about his outlaw uncle; perhaps he was too embarrassed, since his relationship was so much closer than mine is today.

We found out our family's connection to Sundance almost by accident later that year. My uncle, Bill Longabough, Grand-pop's son, was at a church dinner. While waiting in the traditional buffet line, a friend said she wasn't going to stand near him because he had to be related to that outlaw, Harry Longabaugh. After all, it was such an unusual last name, they had to be related. In fact, Longabaugh was my mother's maiden name, and that triggered a series of events and discoveries that for us eventually explained Grandpop's rambling statements.

When Uncle Bill asked what she meant, she explained that she had read an article by Robert Redford on the Outlaw Trail in the *National Geographic*. Redford had portrayed Sundance in the popular 1969 movie *Butch Cassidy and the Sundance Kid*. And in the movie, Redford mentioned that Sundance's real name was Harry Longabaugh. Unfortunately, no one in the family had seen the movie; thus no one had heard that line. But Redford also wrote the name in the article.

Immediately, my uncle started remembering his father's little comments—such as being called "Sundance" as a child, and being told "You had an uncle who robbed banks and trains and died in South America." Grandpop would also say, "He was like Robin Hood; he stole from the rich but gave it away to the poor." We now know Grandpop was wrong on that statement.

Next, Uncle Bill called my wife, Donna, who is the family genealogist and historian. While almost out of breath with excitement, he told her what he suspected. At the Federal Archives, with just a little research in the 1870 and 1880 census, Donna discovered that Sundance appeared on our family tree.

What I quickly discovered truly amazed us all. Sundance and Grandpop's father, Harvey, had been brothers! Furthermore, we had cousins with whom our family branch had lost touch but who knew the family history concerning Sundance. By contacting other family members, particularly the grandson of Sundance's sister Samanna, we started to fill in the missing details.

We arranged a "fun" family reunion that included trading and identifying old family photographs. Suddenly, we were able to put names to four-year-old Sundance with his father Josiah; the heavy-set woman was Annie Place, Sundance's mother; the unidentified but quaint tea party picture was of Butch, Sundance, and his wife, Ethel, in Argentina; and much more.

We found out from family records that as a youth Sundance went west to Illinois and then to Durango, Colorado, with a cousin, George Longenbaugh. George was a horse breeder and Sundance loved working with horses. Sundance's knowledge of fast and reliable horses would serve him well in later years. After he left home in Phoenixville on August 30, 1882, Sundance occasionally would write the family; but he didn't return for a visit until 1900, long after his parents had died.

In 1985, we took our first "Sundance trip" out west; we traveled with our three daughters in a camper. Along the way we started to get hooked on the vast, beautiful scenery along with the haunts in which Sundance lived, worked, and robbed. Reading books such as Charles Kelly's *Outlaw Trail* and James D. Horan's *Desperate Men* sparked our interest to learn more. That began over twenty trips to every place that Sundance rode through. I finally suggested to Donna that she write a book.

The end result was *Sundance, My Uncle,* which was published in 1992. However, in the sixteen years since Donna's first book was published, much new information has come to light about the Sundance Kid. These new revelations helped to complete the story of Sundance.

As we did more and more research, we were astonished at the incomplete accounts and major inaccuracies of the early writings. By using newspapers and first-hand accounts, we were able to fill in many missing pieces within the United States and Canada. Our friends, historians Dan Buck and Anne Meadows, have uncovered the details of Butch and Sundance's South American lives and 1908 deaths in Bolivia. Donna has been able to use information from Anne's book *Digging Up Butch and Sundance* (1994) to detail Sundance's life in South America.

The Pinkertons, railroads, and banks all too quickly accused the Wild Bunch outlaws of every robbery that happened. Anyone in a bowler hat was obviously Butch or Sundance. Many times they were accused of holdups that occurred when they were actually days away from the site or even out of the country. Although wrong in what they did do, they were accused of far more crimes than those they actually committed.

The Wild Bunch, a loose-knit group made up mostly of cowboys, robbed a lot of banks and trains for a living. Butch and Sundance, the gang leaders, preferred outracing a posse rather than having a gunfight. Not until the final shootout in 1908 is there any evidence they ever killed anyone.

Many of the early Wild Bunch writers didn't travel out west or authenticate the stories being reported of Butch and Sundance. By researching the Pinkerton Detective Agency Archives, and visiting museums and libraries out west, Donna has written a more complete and more accurate biography of Sundance's life.

Some examples of new finds and corrections concern the location of the Wilcox, Wyoming, train robbery in 1899. The year following the holdup, the Union Pacific rerouted and straightened the tracks thirty miles south; so the original site is now just an elevated rail bed out on the prairie. Donna also located payroll records in Wyoming, showing that Sundance worked as a cowboy shortly after leaving Colorado and before he started along his outlaw trail. Letters from Dave Gillespie, a Wyoming friend, show that Sundance could not have participated in the Belle Fourche bank robbery of 1897—he was captured later with the real robbers and falsely accused.

Donna discovered new information in Canada that describes Sundance's two years there before returning to the states to rob a train in Montana. We found a note in the Pinkerton files that clears Sundance and Butch of the Tipton, Wyoming, train robbery of August 1900. At that time, they were well on their way to Winnemucca, six hundred miles away, where they made their biggest heist. That money enabled them to prepare for a new life in South America. As for the Winnemucca, Nevada, bank robbery, our detailed following of the escape route found the Idaho ranch, store, and cabin where Sundance stopped. It looks the same today, even to the old hitching post.

Although we like to say that we have uncovered the complete story of Sundance's life, the identity of his wife, Ethel Place, remains a mystery. We have many theories and possibilities, but nothing absolute. She originally came from Texas and apparently met Sundance there, possibly in the late 1890s. They were husband and wife, through the good and the bad, until 1906, when she disappeared from history.

Surely Sundance's life would have been more fulfilling and productive if he had gone straight. We don't approve of the choices he made, but one hundred years later the research has been an enjoyable experience for us and has enabled us to make many new friends along the way.

Acknowledgments

When my husband Paul and I were first married, neither of us had ever heard of the Sundance Kid. But genealogy was my hobby, and we discovered the family skeleton in the fall of 1976. Harry A. Longabaugh, alias the Sundance Kid, was Paul's great, great uncle.

We read books; we traveled west; we researched unpublished manuscripts and court papers; and we visited just about anywhere that ever claimed "Sundance slept here." In short, we were hooked.

But our search never would have been as successful without the help and encouragement of friends we met along the way. Researchers Dan Buck and Anne Meadows discovered letters and depositions in Argentina that help explain and clarify events in South America; and they freely shared their finds with us. A British researcher, Michael Bell, found a newspaper account of the Winnemucca bank robbery written from Sundance's viewpoint; he also looked into the genealogy of a number of British and Welsh families who had immigrated to Argentina. Dan Davidson, curator of the Museum of Northwest Colorado, obtained letters and memoirs from descendants of Sundance's friends along the Little Snake River Valley and put us in contact with relatives of these families.

Harry A. Longabaugh, age four, with his father Josiah. © Paul D. Ernst.

But my highest appreciation goes to my family, my most patient and biggest support system during thirty years of "Sundance mania." Thanks go to my husband, who gave his vacations over for research trips, donated hours to reading despite tired eyes, and was persistent in his search for the full truth about his uncle. Thanks also belong to our three daughters—Jennifer, Susan, and Janice—who were patient, supportive, and encouraging during their growing-up years. And my gratitude goes to my sister, Derri Benbow, for her editing and advice.

Finally, speaking briefly for the Longabough descendants, we neither condone nor make excuses for Sundance's life. He wanted easy money, plain and simple. And, contrary to Grandpop's comments, Sundance was never like Robin Hood. As wrong as he may have been, however, he was our Uncle Harry; and we wanted to share, through this new book, what we know of Sundance. We hope it will allow you, the reader, to understand him better.

THE
SUNDANCE
KID

CHAPTER 1

The Wild Bunch

From cattle rustling to bank robberies and train holdups—that often seemed to be a natural progression of events with some cowboys during the late nineteenth century. The gangs of cowboys-turned-outlaws shared in the stolen money and excitement found along the Outlaw Trail, a series of hideouts and safe houses, in the Old West.

The Wild Bunch was one of the best-known outlaw gangs in Old West history, well trained and experienced in travel along the Outlaw Trail. Their name came about as a result of their frequent wild behavior in towns along the Wyoming, Colorado, and Utah borders. They shot up saloons and hurrahed main streets in celebration, earning themselves recognition as a wild bunch of cowboys in the local newspapers. The name stuck.

The Wild Bunch had a loose membership of about twenty-five men, but any given robbery seldom involved more than two or three of the same men from any previous or future holdup. Their biggest advantage over the law was their skill in keeping their identities uncertain, their use of good horse-flesh and relays, and their ability to lie low in one of the hideouts between heists. The core group consisted of five men.

The leader of the gang was Robert LeRoy Parker, alias Butch Cassidy. The oldest of thirteen children, Butch was born April 13, 1866, in Beaver, Utah, to a pioneering Mormon family. His early mentor was Mike Cassidy, a hired hand and sometime rustler from a neighboring ranch. When the necessity to pick an alias became apparent, Parker became Cassidy. Except for his penchant for stealing money, Butch adhered to a rather strict code of conduct. He never killed anyone until the end; and it has been said that he never stole from the common people, just from banks and railroads.

Harvey Alexander Logan, alias Kid Curry, was born in 1867 in Tama County, Iowa, the third of six children. After the deaths of his parents, he and his three brothers homesteaded in Landusky, Montana, where they made a living rustling cattle and horses. But ranching was too mild for Harvey's temperament. He was the wildest member of the gang—he murdered nine men—but he deferred to Butch's leadership in the gang's escapades.

Benjamin Arnold Kilpatrick, alias the Tall Texan, was born in 1874 in Coleman County, Texas. The family of ten children moved to a ranch in Tom Green County, Texas, where Ben and his brothers quickly earned a reputation as the delinquents of the day. Two of his earliest acquaintances were Sam and Tom Ketchum, fellow Texans and future outlaw leaders.

William Richard Carver, alias Will Causey, was born September 12, 1868, in Wilson County, Texas. Originally a member of the Texas-based Ketchum brothers gang, he did not join the Wild Bunch until the Ketchum gang began to break up. Will was probably the only member of the Wild Bunch who could stand his own against the marksmanship of Sundance.

Harry Alonzo Longabaugh was born in the spring of 1867 in Mont Clare, Pennsylvania, the youngest of five children. In 1887, he was sentenced to eighteen months in jail for stealing a horse in Sundance, Wyoming. Having earned an outlaw reputation and the alias the Sundance Kid, he quickly became proficient at both bank and train robberies. He and Butch became partners and eventually tried to go straight in South America. This is his story . . .

CHAPTER 2

The Early Years
Phoenixville, Pennsylvania

By today's standards, Harry Alonzo Longabaugh's family seems almost dysfunctional. Saying that, however, does not in any way pardon or excuse the decisions he made throughout his life. Whatever he made of his early life was done purely for excitement and easy money, and he paid dearly for his behavior. But his upbringing may help explain his choices.

The Longabaugh family lived along the Schuylkill River and Canal in the neighboring towns of Mont Clare, Montgomery County, and Phoenixville, Chester County, Pennsylvania.[1] Their ancestor Conrad Langenbach emigrated from Germany as an indentured servant, arriving in Philadelphia on December 24, 1772, aboard the brig *Morning Star*.[2] Conrad's debt was released early, just in time for him to serve with the Northampton County Militia during the Revolutionary War. At the end of his service, Conrad settled in eastern Pennsylvania, about thirty miles north of Philadelphia. By the time he married Catharina in 1781, his surname had been through a variety of spellings and was phonetically Anglicized to Longabaugh. The Longabaugh union was blessed with seven children, the last one named Jonas Isaac, born in 1798 in Pennsylvania.

122 Jacobs Street, Mont Clare, where Sundance was born

Jonas Longabaugh married Christiana Hillbert in 1821, and they had five children—Josiah, Nathaniel, Michael, Mary, and Margaret; a sixth baby was stillborn. Josiah, the oldest, was born June 14, 1822, in Montgomery County, Pennsylvania; he married Annie G. Place, the daughter of Deacon Henry and Rachel (Tustin) Place, on August 11, 1855, in Phoenixville. They also had five children—Elwood Place, born June 21, 1858; Samanna, born April 22, 1860; Emma T., born in 1863; Harvey Sylvester, born May 19, 1865; and Harry Alonzo, born in the spring of 1867.[3]

Josiah was not particularly ambitious; he never owned property or held a job for any length of time.[4] He was drafted for service in the Civil War and was later granted a pension for "General Debility," a gentle way of saying that he had hemorrhoids.[5] Annie, however, worked hard to make a home for her family; she was very religious and very strict.

For years, the family moved from one rented house to another, almost annually. They seemed to move each time Josiah changed jobs, from day laborer to carpenter to farm hand; but they always stayed in the neighboring towns of Mont Clare and Phoenixville. When Harry was born, the family was living in half of a duplex located at 122 Jacobs Street in Mont Clare.[6] The duplex backed up to the Schuyl-kill Canal, on which Josiah was then working.

The towns of Phoenixville and Mont Clare were very blue collar with a large mix of Italian, Irish, and German immi-grants.[7] Phoenixville, the home of the Phoenix Iron Company, was very much a mill town. The company board members also served as officers of the "Iron Bank." They donated a large tract of land for a town park; they underwrote a general store for employees only; they bought out a failing nail manufac-turing company to save local jobs; and they donated free family housing to workers who volunteered to serve in the Union.

In contrast to the ethnic mix of laborers was the impres-sive leadership at the Phoenix Iron Company, which included future politicians such as Governor Samuel Pennypacker, inven-tors such as John Griffen, and military men.[8] Beginning in 1861, the Phoenix began manufacturing "the Griffen wrought iron cannon, an arm made by welding together bars laid longitudi-nally, transversely and spirally, and which, on trial in the field, proved to be peculiarly durable and effective. About twelve hundred of these guns were supplied" to the United States government. As the Griffen gun "gained the reputation of being the best arm of the kind in the service and were more generally used in the light artillery than any other" weapon, it also reflected well upon the town of Phoenixville. Both the town and the company prospered.

Although none of the Longabaugh family members are known to have worked for the Phoenix, the atmosphere in such a company town influenced everyone. Just half a mile away, across the covered bridge from Phoenixville, the village of Mont Clare was a boatman's community. While a few of the local residents walked over to the mills, the majority worked along the canal. Because Josiah worked on the canal, it was the influence that affected the Longabaugh family the most strongly. Originally built to facilitate the shipping of coal from upstate Pennsylvania to Philadelphia, the canal also serviced local communities for shipment of farm products and iron.

Harry's Uncle Michael, who owned a large home in Mont Clare, had his own canal boats and merchandised the products he shipped out of a small store in Phoenixville. He often carried the coal and other local products to ports as distant as Boston, New York, Erie, and Scranton. At one time or another, the Longabaugh brothers, including Harry, each worked for Uncle Michael, prodding the mules along the canal and poling the boats on the river.

According to the 1880 federal census records, by the time Harry and his brother Harvey were teenagers, Josiah had sent them out of the home to work; they were hired servants, boarding with their employers.[9] Samanna had already married and was out of the home, but Elwood and Emma were unemployed and living at home. No one today seems to know why the older siblings stayed at home, while the two younger boys were earning their keep elsewhere.

The census records indicate that Harry, age thirteen, was boarding with the Wilmer Ralston family in West Vincent Township, Chester County, about ten miles from his parents. Ralston owned over one hundred acres of farmland and raised horses. It was at the Ralstons that young Harry first worked with horses, a trade that proved quite useful in later years.

By 1882, Harry had moved back home with his parents, who were then living at 354 Church Street in Phoenixville.

354 Church Street, Phoenixville, Pennsylvania

He attended the First Baptist Church in Phoenixville, where the family worshipped and where his maternal grandfather, Henry Place, was a respected deacon; and he attended the nearby Gay Street School just three blocks away. In spite of his sporadic schooling, Harry was well read—he owned his own library card, purchased at the cost of $1 and issued on January 31, 1881. He probably began reading novels about the exciting and wild West.

Harry's oldest brother, Elwood, left home in 1882 and became a whaler aboard the *Mary & Helen* out of Maine and bound for California, probably via Cape Horn. Elwood was based out of the San Francisco Bay area, and the Pinkerton Detective Agency recorded that, in later years, Harry and Elwood were frequently in contact with each other.[10]

Samanna, his oldest sister, was married to Oliver Hallman, a self-employed, wrought-iron worker who had apprenticed

Elwood Place
Longabaugh

under John Griffen, and they had already begun a family. In his youth, Harry and Samanna had developed a close and long-lasting relationship; she was the sibling who stayed most in touch with him over the years. In fact, the Pinkerton Detective Agency recorded her home address in their files and paid a postal clerk to open her mail and watch her home from the Mont Clare post office a few doors away.

The Pinkertons were in themselves an interesting story. The Pinkerton Detective Agency began as the North Western Police Agency in Chicago, Illinois, in 1850 under the direction of Allan Pinkerton. Pinkerton was born on August 25, 1819, in Glasgow, Scotland, and immigrated to the United States in 1842 in order to avoid an arrest warrant. He had been an agitator for workers' rights in Scotland, and immediately picked up the abolitionists' cause in the States, aiding many runaway slaves in reaching Canada.[11]

Using his new agency, Pinkerton also worked closely with the railroads to capture holdup men and to organize a guard force on board the trains. During the 1850s, he made a name for himself doing railroad undercover work. Then, in February 1861, Pinkerton discovered a plot to assassinate President-elect Lincoln. Soon thereafter, President Lincoln asked Pinkerton, using the alias of Major E. J. Allen, to close the North Western Police Agency and to set up a Union spy system for the government. In later years, this same system became the Federal Secret Service, which in turn served as a primary concept for the Federal Bureau of Investigation.

After the Civil War, Pinkerton opened a new agency, named Pinkerton's National Detective Agency, which used an open eye for its logo and the motto "We never sleep." He took fierce pride in his work and accomplishments and once wrote, "I do not know the meaning of the word 'fail.' Nothing in hell or heaven can influence me when I know that I am right."[12]

However, it was this certitude that put Pinkerton's methods on the border of unethical. With Pinkerton's death in 1884, his sons William and Robert really pushed legal methods to the limit. In a 1921 letter William A. Pinkerton wrote, "We did have to do with the breaking up of the 'Wild Bunch' and the killing off of a number of them." Another unsigned letter stated, "We hope someday to apprehend these people in this country or through our correspondents get them killed in the Argentine Republic."[13] They became desperate in their cause; they wanted these outlaws at any cost.

Expenses for the Pinkertons were usually paid by the American Bankers Association, the Union Pacific Railroad, the Great Northern Railroad, and other large companies. However, "on one occasion at the agency's expense . . . [Pinkertons] sent an official from the New York Office to the Argentine Republic to endeavor to get information and locate the remaining members of this band. . . . The American Bankers

FORM 55-3-'01-10M-AE.

P. N. D. A. ....No. 1961

NAME......Harry Longbaugh.   No. 470 R
ALIAS......."Kid" Longbaugh; Harry Alonzo;.
    Frank Jones; Frank Boyd; the "Sundance
    Kid"
NATIVITY..Swedish-American. COLOR..White.
OCCUPATION...............Cowboy; rustler
CRIMINAL OCCUPATION.........Highwayman,
    bank burglar, cattle and horse thief
AGE......35 years.   HEIGHT......5 ft, 10 in
WEIGHT......165 to 175 lbs. BUILD...Good.
EYES....Blue or gray. NOSE....Rather long
COMPLEXION......................Medium
STYLE OF BEARD.........Mustache, (if any),
    natural color brown, reddish tinge
FEATURES..........................Grecian type.
COLOR OF HAIR ...Natural color brown, may
    be dyed; combs it pompadour
IS BOW-LEGGED; FEET FAR APART.
REMARKS :—Harry Longbaugh served 18
    months in jail at Sundance, Cook Co.,
    Wyoming, when a boy, for horse stealing.
    In December, 1892, Harry Longbaugh,
    Bill Madden and Henry Bass "held up" a
    Great Northern train at Malta, Montana.
    Bass and Madden were tried for this
    crime, convicted and sentenced to 10 and
    14 years respectively; Longbaugh es-
    caped and since has been a fugitive. June
    28, 1897, under the name of Frank Jones,
    Longbaugh participated with Harvey
    Logan, alias Curry, Tom Day and Walter
    Putney, in the Belle Fourche, South
    Dakota, bank robbery. All were arrested,
    but Longbaugh and Harvey Logan escaped
    from jail at Deadwood, October 31, the
    same year. Wanted for robbery First
    National Bank, Winnemucca, Nevada, Sep-
    tember 19th, 1900. See Information No.
    421.

Pinkerton's identification card for Sundance

Association would not permit the expense. And therefore we have been keeping a run on these people in our own way."[14]

Keeping track in *their own way* meant the hiring of undercover detectives and the paying of informants. Paid informants included postal clerks who were expected to open mail and forward information to the agency. One of their best undercover agents, Charlie Siringo, managed to infiltrate the gang under the guise of a fugitive from Texas.[15] Siringo gleaned much family information from Harvey Logan's family in Montana and from Sundance's friends in Wyoming. His reports became part of the dossiers that the agency opened on each Wild Bunch outlaw.

Also listed in these Pinkerton files was Harry's sister Emma, who became a successful businesswoman in a day when

Samanna and Emma Longabaugh

women's rights and independence were rare. By the 1890s, she owned a seamstress business, McCandless and Longabaugh, which did piecework for the well-known John Wanamaker's Department Store in Philadelphia. Family members remember Emma as a spinster and as the most austere member of the family. She eventually changed the spelling of her name

Harvey Sylvester Longabaugh

to Longabough because having an outlaw for a brother was not good for business. But the Pinkertons knew where she lived and worked and entered the information into their growing dossier on her brother.

Harry's brother Harvey was a day laborer and carpenter like their father, and his business sign is still owned by the family today. The Pinkerton Detective Agency records show that in 1902 Harry visited the beach resort in Atlantic City, New Jersey, at a time when Harvey was doing carpentry work on the now-famous Boardwalk.

At the age of fourteen, Harry traveled by canal boat with his Uncle Michael to find a new job. His sister Samanna kept the business books for her husband and made occasional personal notations among the purchase orders. She wrote, "Phoenixville June 1882—Harry A. Longabaugh left home to seek employment in Ph. [Philadelphia]. And from their [*sic*] to N.Y.C. from their [*sic*] to Boston and from their [*sic*] home on the 26 of July or near that date."[16]

However, he was apparently unsuccessful because Samanna's next entry reads, "Phoenixville Aug. 30th 1882 Harry A. Longabaugh left home for the West. Left home at 14 [years old]—Church St. Phoenixville below Gay St."[17] Harry boarded the train at the Phoenixville depot less than a mile from his home. He traveled alone, past Horseshoe Curve in western Pennsylvania, and headed for the West he had read about so often.

Harry left home to help a distant cousin, George Longenbaugh, who had just taken his pregnant wife, Mary, and young son, Walter, from Illinois to Colorado by covered wagon.[18]

CHAPTER 3

Ranching in Cortez, Colorado

George Longenbaugh descended from Baltzer and Elizabeth Lanabach, a branch of Conrad's family. Baltzer's lineage traveled from Germany to Baltimore, Maryland, and eventually moved through Shelbyville, Ohio, and into Shelby County, Illinois. In 1882 George needed Harry to help settle the new homestead.[1]

According to George's descendants today, George originally moved his family to Durango, Colorado, where he worked with the town's new irrigation system, and the family settled into their new home. However, within a year George decided to move about fifty miles farther west to Cortez as land opened for homesteading, and he invited Harry to join them. Harry remained with George and his family until early 1886, helping with the horses and the new homestead. Together they bred horses, planted a few crops to feed the family, and made the necessary improvements on the land.

Harry also worked occasionally for Henry Goodman, the foreman of the LC Ranch in nearby McElmo Canyon. During Harry's time with cousin George, he became a horse wrangler and learned how to purchase and breed good horseflesh, trades he would put to good use in the future.

The town of Cortez also provided Harry with an opportunity to meet some of his future outlaw partners. The Madden brothers lived in Mancos, within less than a day's ride from the Longenbaugh ranch in Cortez. Bill Madden partnered with Harry for a train robbery in Malta, Montana, in 1892.[2] Outlaw Tom McCarty had a ranch hideout less than a mile from the Longenbaugh family ranch; in fact, Mary Longenbaugh was known to provide perishable food, such as eggs and butter, when Tom was hiding in the sagebrush and cedars.[3]

Cortez was also just about seventy-five miles from the growing mining town of Telluride, Colorado. At the time, Telluride was the home of both Willard Erastus Christiansen, later known as Matt Warner, and Robert LeRoy Parker, alias Butch Cassidy. Together Butch, Matt, and Tom often raced horses in McElmo Canyon and in Telluride.[4]

Although it is not certain exactly when or where young Harry actually met these outlaws, at least two possible occasions occurred near Cortez while Harry lived there with George's family. While working for the LC Ranch, Harry often had reason to ride herd in the open range of McElmo Canyon. Horse races were frequently held in the canyon, and it seems likely that he may have attended at least a race or two in McElmo. One race developed into a major incident.

McCarty, Warner, and Cassidy had already won in many area towns when they brought a mare named Betty into McElmo to race a one-eyed Indian pony named White Face.[5] When Betty easily won, the Utes willingly handed over their blankets but refused to give up White Face as agreed. Tom beat one of the Indians with his quirt, grabbed the reins on White Face's neck, and raced away. After hiding overnight at McCarty's ranch at Cortez, the winners were awakened by Indians attempting to reclaim their horse. At least one shot was fired, killing an Indian, before the fight broke up. The Indians departed with their dead companion, and Tom,

Matt, and Butch quickly returned to Telluride with Betty and White Face.

The second opportunity for meeting involved a minor dispute between Henry Goodman's ranch hands and the herders working for the rival Carlisle Ranch in nearby Monticello, Utah. Harry was working for Goodman at the time, and Dan Parker, younger brother of Butch Cassidy, was working for the Carlisle.[6] Some Goodman sheep were stolen and slaughtered, and the hides hung out to dry; one report claims Parker was the culprit. When Carlisle happened upon the skins, he angrily told his foreman, Len Scott, to hide them out of sight in an old cabin in town.

Later, a Goodman ranch hand, in town for a local dance, noticed the skins and reported the theft to Goodman. However, Parker reportedly saw what was happening, and he quickly switched the Goodman hides for some with the Carlisle brand. When Goodman arrived on the scene, he saw only Carlisle skins, and he immediately ordered their return, bringing the confusing situation to an angry end. Both Harry and Dan Parker may very well have been involved, and Harry could have met Dan and his brother Butch.

In any event, by 1886 Harry was anxious to strike out on his own. He left Cortez and headed north.

CHAPTER 4

The Outlaw Trail

The Hole in the Wall, Brown's Park, Powder Springs, and Robbers Roost were all major hideouts along the Outlaw Trail. Connected by a winding, roaming, and unmarked cattle trail that ran from the Canadian border to the Mexican border, the hideouts provided safety between jobs and over the winter. For the most part, they were well-known by the outlaws and unbothered by the law.

The Hole in the Wall was originally used by rustlers for herding stolen cattle and horses. The Hole was located about sixteen miles from Kaycee, Wyoming, so-named for the KC Ranch owned by rustler Nate Champion, who was killed during the Johnson County Cattle War of 1892. Although hideout cabins were scattered about the area, there never was an actual town behind the steep, red sandstone canyon wall; the area was originally a desolate, dry, ancient riverbed. Neither was there a "hole" in the canyon wall; rather, there was a narrow notch through which horses and cattle could be run. It was often said that the outlaws and rustlers could see for miles in any direction from the top of the wall, and that just a few men could hold off a posse of one hundred men if necessary.

Flatnose George Sutherland Currie headed a small gang of cattle rustlers who worked out of the Hole in the Wall. He

The Hole in the Wall today

was originally part of the Red Sash Gang that headquartered in Kaycee, but he eventually began to hold up banks with Harvey Logan and other lesser-known Wild Bunch gang members. It was in the Hole in the Wall that Sundance likely met Flatnose George Currie. Certainly he would also have spent time there with Harvey Logan and Butch Cassidy.

In her history of the Hole in the Wall, local historian Thelma Gatchell wrote, "Longabaugh like Cassidy was happy-go-lucky, courageous and liked by all who knew him. He was also tall, good looking and dark complexioned with a smart mustache, very temperate in his drinking, and never a killer. It was said that Cassidy, Logan, and Longabaugh were the 'Big Trio' of the Hole in the Wall gang."[1]

A two- or three-day ride from the Hole is Brown's Park, a forty-mile by six-mile valley that straddles the tristate corners of Wyoming, Colorado, and Utah. Located on the Green River and surrounded by Douglas, Diamond, and Cold Spring mountains, it was already a populated valley during the era of the outlaws. It offered mild winters, good grazing, and state lines that raised invisible barriers against pursuit from the law. Many outlaws, including Sundance, found occasional ranch work with the friendly ranch families who lived in the Park.

As long as a reputed outlaw earned his keep and behaved himself locally, he was a welcome addition. One local story tells of the Outlaws' Thanksgiving Dinner around 1895.[2] Sundance, Butch, and a few other outlaws played host to the community; they prepared and served a complete, traditional turkey dinner. The local families brought their finest linens, dishes, and silver for the meal and even arrived dressed in their Sunday best.

Sundance greeted the guests at the hitching post of the Davenport Ranch on Willow Creek. Once the guests had all arrived, he and Butch put on white butcher aprons and served their guests an elegant dinner. The party lasted into the wee hours of the morning with local entertainment and dancing.

Ann Bassett, a young teen at the time, later claimed that Sundance was tall, blond, and handsome, and that he had the young girls thoroughly enchanted the entire evening.[3]

Just over Douglas Mountain was the homestead of Willard Erastus Christiansen, alias Matt Warner, one of the men who held up the bank in Telluride in 1889.[4] His land bordered the hideout known as Powder Springs in Wyoming. Sundance knew Powder Springs quite well because he spent about two years working less than forty miles away for Al Reader of Savery, Wyoming. Even closer was the Reader Cabin Draw, where Sundance kept the Reader herd during the winter months. A local newspaper wrote, "Reader's outfit left last Monday for the lower country for the winter. Bert Charter, Harry Alonzo, and Mr. Filbrick were with the horses."[5]

Powder Springs was originally a safe stopover for local rustlers, but Butch Cassidy's Wild Bunch used it a great deal during the late 1890s. The hideout is actually made up of the upper and lower springs, both of which housed outlaw cabins at one time. The surrounding area is sagebrush and dust, but the springs are lush and green.

Besides its ideal location between the Hole in the Wall and Brown's Park, Powder Springs also offered a visible marker of safety. Powder Springs happens to be within sight of Wyoming State Mile Marker no. 223, which was placed along the forty-first parallel when the boundary between the Territory of Wyoming and the future state of Colorado was surveyed in August of 1873. That five-foot marker provided a clear definition of safety to those hiding at the springs; it meant the law could not reach them. The Springs became much more popular with the gang after the law invaded the Hole in the Wall in July 1897.

The last major hideout along the Outlaw Trail was Robbers Roost, located in the high desert canyons of Utah, about midway between Moab and Hanksville. Away from the Green River or the Colorado River, which border the Roost, there

Powder Springs hideout today

is a serious lack of water in the area. The Roost's intimidating and twisting canyons protected the outlaws by keeping the law out. One lawman who was foolish enough to venture into the Roost was Sheriff Tom Fares.[6]

He followed Tom McCarty, Matt Warner, and Butch Cassidy into the Roost, and lost his way in the dry maze of canyons. Matt got the drop on him, gave him a water canteen, and headed him out of the Roost. However, Fares was overheard threatening to return to *get his man,* which made Matt and the others angry. They then took Fares' saddle and pants and sent him riding towards Hanksville in just his under-drawers and riding bareback. Robbers Roost was considered to be the most inhospitable of the Outlaw Trail hideouts.

With its proximity to his cousin's home in Cortez, Colorado, Sundance may have known the Roost before learning of the other stops on the trail. And Butch Cassidy's mentor, Mike Cassidy, was said to have run his rustled cattle through the Roost on many occasions.

One of the minor stops along the Outlaw Trail was the area of Malta and Culbertson, Montana, just below the Canadian border. Located where the N Bar N range in Montana met the badlands of Canada, it was an area where both Sundance and Harvey Logan ran with a local rustler gang.[7]

Dutch Henry Ieuch led a gang of rustlers and often partnered activities with the Nelson–Jones Gang, under the leadership of Frank Jones. The headquarters for both gangs was just north of Culbertson, which was convenient for frequent forays into Canada. In later years, Sundance often used the name Frank Jones as an alias. In June of 1900, J. D. B. Grieg, an informant from Malta, Montana, wrote the Pinkerton Detective Agency to complain about the number of outlaws living near Culbertson.

Grieg wrote, "About Culbertson there are a couple of fellows, ex-cowboys . . . [who] formerly worked for the N–N outfit that are outlaws and fugitives from justice. There is

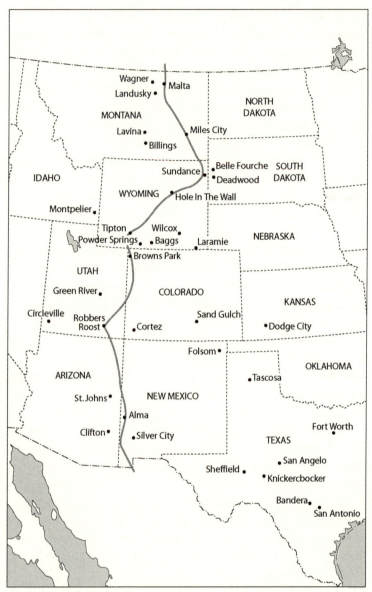

Map of the Outlaw Trail

another party named Logenbough [*sic*] who was supposed to have been implicated in the holdup which occurred at Malta a number of years ago. Some people here think he is one of the Jones or Roberts boys. . . . They rustle cattle and horses, do many misdeeds and either hide in Canada or across the border."[8] Grieg was the editor of the *Harlem Enterprise* and also knew the Logan boys, although he claimed not to know of their illegal activities.

Near the Mexican border was a final stop that was not normally considered a hideout but that was definitely part of the Outlaw Trail. The W S Ranch in Alma, New Mexico, was run by Captain William French, who did not originally know that a number of his ranch hands were members of Butch Cassidy's Wild Bunch. He only knew that when Jim Lowe, an alias used by Butch, was around, his herds were not rustled and his ranch was well run.[9] Therefore, whenever any of Butch's friends arrived looking for work, French gladly hired them.[10] After the Wilcox train robbery in 1899, Pinkerton agent Frank Murray was sent down to Alma on the trail of stolen loot. Captain French claimed utter surprise at the charge that one of his best hands was actually an outlaw; but it certainly explained the almost constant comings and goings of Butch and other ranch hands.

The W S Ranch was located near the Arizona state line and was not overly far from Mexico, which made it a safe haven for outlaws on the run. Furthermore, it was less than a two days' ride to the railroad in either Magdalena or Silver City, New Mexico. The railroads and nearby state boundaries provided quick and easy escapes to outlaws on the run.

CHAPTER 5

The Suffolk Cattle Company

After leaving his cousin in Cortez, nineteen-year-old Harry drifted north through Colorado and into Wyoming and took work wherever he could find it. Spring was a good time to find new work for experienced horse wranglers. Cattle needed to be rounded up, counted, and branded. Good wranglers were needed to care for a remuda of horses for the cowhands. More horses were always needed, and breaking them was hard and dangerous work; however, it was what Harry enjoyed doing and it paid well.

On April 20, 1886, Harry was hired at the pay rate of $35 per month by the Suffolk Cattle Company of Crook County (now Weston County), Wyoming.[1] The ranch was located about thirty miles northwest of the town of Lusk, where another distant cousin of Harry's was then living.

Ellsworth Eugene Lonabaugh (usually called E. E.) had the same grandfather as George Longenbaugh and was Harry's fourth cousin. E. E. was a close friend of the town's founding father, Frank Lusk. Together, E. E. and Frank had worked the local mines and laid out a town that was founded in 1886. E. E. then hung out his shingle, advertising himself as the local lawyer. However, an incident involving Harry may have hastened E. E.'s departure for the growing city of Sheridan, Wyoming.

According to a letter written by Sam W. Mather, a coworker at the Suffolk Cattle Company at the time, Harry was a hot-headed youngster. "In the eighties I was working for the Suffolk Cattle Co., of Wyoming. Their ranch, the A V, was located on the Cheyenne river at the mouth of Lodge Pole. . . . a boy about 18 years old, came to the ranch hunting work; he said his name was Harry Longbaugh [sic] and that he was from Colorado. Our foreman, J. B. Crawford, put him to wrangling horses, and the first week on the round-up he whipped three horse wranglers about the best grazing ground for our remuda, and came very near whipping our Dutch cook for calling him Longboy. After that the cooks and horse-wranglers did not step on his toes. He got on fine until we got back to the ranch, when the sheriff from Lusk, Wyoming, arrested him for robbing an old man of $80, but he got away that night. . . ."[2]

Although Mather's letter indicates that Harry worked for the Suffolk Company for a few weeks, Crawford issued Harry a check for $1.25, the equivalent of one day's work, on April 21, 1886. No explanation is shown in ranch records for Harry's immediate departure, but a robbery would certainly be reason enough for dismissal.

CHAPTER 6

The N Bar N Ranch

The Home Land & Cattle Company, also known as the N Bar N, had its start on September 15, 1885, as a Missouri company owned by brothers William F. and Frederick G. Niedringhaus. Their entry into the growing cattle business was an extension of their St. Louis enamelware manufacturing company and Utah silver mining ventures.[1]

Already successful businessmen, the brothers used their surplus capital to purchase the Anchor THL Ranch, located near Miles City, Montana, from Major Thomas H. Logan of Fort Keough, Wyoming. The brothers chose their initials N–N as their main brand, to signify the close relationship between the two men; and the ranch was called N Bar N.

The N Bar N began with about 6,000 head of cattle and used the open range from Wolf Point and Rock Creek in northern Montana south to their headquarters at Miles City. The company eventually owned ranches spread from Saskatchewan, Canada, to Clayton, New Mexico, all under the banner of the N Bar N Ranch. Soon a third brother, H. L. Niedringhaus, was brought into the business to oversee the purchasing of both horses and cattle for the company. By the end of 1886, the N Bar N reported 65,000 cattle on their northern range.

The N Bar N Ranch. Photograph by Albert W. Niedringhaus, courtesy of the Niedringhaus Family.

During that 1886 expansion, a drive of 17,000 cattle trailed north from Perico Creek, New Mexico, to Little Dry Creek, Montana. Harry A. Longabaugh was listed in the employee records of the N Bar N at this time.

But Harry's timing was bad—the harsh winter of 1886–87 became known as "The Big Die Up." The N Bar N lost between 20,000 and 40,000 head of cattle to the freezing ice and snow, and a number of cowboys were laid off, including Harry. The Niedringhaus brothers hung on, but just barely.

According to a letter he wrote later, Harry drifted to the Black Hills of South Dakota, where he worked for food and shelter, but little else. "I have always worked for an honest living; was employed last summer by one of the best outfits in Montana and don't think they can say aught against me, but having got discharged last winter I went to the Black Hills to seek employment—which I could not get—and was forced to work for my board a month and a half, rather than to beg or steal. I finally started back to the vicinity of Miles City, as it was spring, to get employment on the range."[2]

Harry was headed back to the N Bar N Ranch hoping for work when he ran into trouble on the V V V (Three V) Ranch. It was a decision that changed his life forever.

CHAPTER 7

Robbery on the Three V Ranch

The Three V Ranch, so-called for its V V V brand, was located in the northeastern corner of the state of Wyoming and touched the borders of South Dakota and Montana. The road Harry traveled between South Dakota's Black Hills and the N Bar N crossed right through the heart of the Three V.

The Three V horse camp and winter quarters were located on Crow Creek in an area of canyons and wide-open range just north of the town of Sundance, Wyoming. Although no longer part of the Three V, a small ranch still sits in the canyon, and one of the original cabins is used as a local community building.[1]

During the winter and spring of 1887, the Three V Ranch, also known as Western Ranches Ltd., was owned by a group of English investors and was under the management of John Clay and his assistant, Robert Robinson. Clay was very respected and influential in the area; he was a member of the exclusive Cheyenne Club, and he was voted president of the well-known Wyoming Stock Growers Association.

On February 27, 1887, as Harry headed back to the N Bar N, he stole a light grey horse branded *J* on the left shoulder, a revolver, and a saddle outfit from Alonzo Craven of the Three V Ranch. He continued northwest toward Miles

City, while the employees of the Three V began a search for a "smooth-faced, grey-eyed boy" in possession of the stolen goods.[2]

After unsuccessfully searching for two weeks, James Widner, an employee of the Three V rode into Sundance, Wyoming, the Crook County seat. Because the Three V Ranch sat on the border of Montana, South Dakota, and Wyoming, Widner opted for the closest county seat. On March 15, 1887, Widner filed charges with Sheriff James Ryan on behalf of himself and Alonzo Craven.

Ryan soon received word that Harry had been picked up outside Miles City. According to the *Sundance Gazette*, "Sheriff Ryan has gone to Miles City after the kid who stole Jim Widner's horse, on the head of Crow Creek in this county. He was caught there some time ago."[3] On April 8, 1887, Ryan filed arrest papers in Miles City and temporarily housed Harry in the small jail located on the north side of the new court-house, located at Main and Seventh Streets.[4]

On April 12th, for reasons unknown and confusing, Ryan took young Harry to St. Paul, Minnesota, nearly 700 miles away, on board the Northern Pacific Railroad. Even the newspaper commented on the unusual route. "Sheriff Ryan departed with the prisoner this morning bound for Sundance. The route taken by the sheriff would seem to be a long one; Miles City to St. Paul. St. Paul to the railroad terminus in the Black Hills and thence by stage to Sundance, a distance in all of nearly 2,000 miles. Sundance is less than 300 miles across country from here."[5]

Having reached St. Paul, Ryan and Harry turned around and headed west to Rapid City, South Dakota, again by train. But somewhere near Duluth, Minnesota, Harry picked the locks of his shackles, slipped out of his handcuffs, and jumped off the moving train while Ryan was in the bathroom.[6] It was suggested that Harry had an accomplice; and some researchers suspect that Butch Cassidy was in the Miles City area at this time, having come north from Wyoming about 1886.[7] However, as will be seen, Harry managed to pick locks and to escape handcuffs without help frequently over the years.[8]

Ryan had the train stopped and searched the immediate area to no avail. When he arrived back in Wyoming, he immediately offered a $250 reward. Ryan may have been frustrated, but Harry was foolish; he returned to the Miles City area. Deputy Sheriff Eph K. Davis and Stock Inspector W. Smith caught up with Harry on June 6th, on the N Bar Ranch in Powderville, Montana. The N Bar, owned by the Newman brothers, was a neighboring ranch to the N Bar N, owned by the Niedringhaus brothers, and Harry likely knew it well. According to the *Big Horn Sentinel,* "Lombaugh [*sic*], the man who escaped from Sheriff Ryan of Sundance . . . [was] arrested at the Newman ranch, on Powder river."[9]

Davis and Smith handcuffed Longabaugh and shackled him to the wall of an N Bar line shack while they waited for the next stage to come through. The regular stage route between Miles City and Deadwood went right past the line shack. It was there, on the N Bar Ranch, according to the newspaper, that Harry again picked the locks and the story of Davis "playing possum" took place.[10]

On Saturday Deputy Sheriff Davis, together with Stock Inspector Smith, made a most important arrest. . . near the N-bar ranch on Powder river. . . After his escape from Sheriff Ryan he [Longabaugh] made his way back to Montana. . . . After Mr. Davis had made the arrest he took three six-shooters from the bold young criminal and shackled him and handcuffed him with some patent lock bracelets which were warranted to hold anything until unlocked by the key and which the manufacturers offered a premium if they could be opened otherwise. Eph Davis had heard a good deal of Longabaugh's prowess in effecting escape, and after taking all due precautions when night closed in upon them he lay down in one corner of a shack and Mr. Smith another, the kid between them. Smith was tired out and soon fell to sleep and Davis played "possum," keeping an eye on the prisoner. Soon as he thought everyone was asleep the kid, shackled and manacled as he was, managed to free himself and rising stealthily approached the window and raised it and was about to make a break for liberty when sly old Eph thought it was time for him to take a hand and raising on his elbow with a cocked six-shooter in his hand he said in a quiet tone of voice, "Kid, your loose, ain't you?" and then called to Smith. The kid dropped back as though he was shot and it is needless to add that the officers did not sleep at the same time during the rest of the night.[11]

Taking offense at the extent of the accusations, Harry wrote a letter to the editor of the newspaper, which published his response on June 9th.

In your issue of the 7th inst. I read a very sensational and partly untrue article, which places me before the public not even second to the notorious Jesse James. Admitting that I have done wrong and expecting to be dealt with according to law and not by false reports from parties who should blush with shame to make them, I ask a little of your space to set my case before the public in a true light. In the first place I have always worked for an honest living; was employed last summer by one of the best outfits in Montana and don't think they can say aught against me, but having got discharged last winter I went to the Black Hills to seek employment—which I could not get— and was forced to work for my board a month and a

Annie G. Place
Longabaugh

half, rather than to beg or steal. . . . I am aware that
some of your readers will say my statement should be
taken for what it is worth, on account of the hard
name which has been forced upon me, nevertheless
it is true. As for my recapture by Deputy Sheriff
Davis, all I can say is that he did his work well and
were it not for his "playing 'possum" I would now be
on my way south, where I had hoped to go and live a
better life.

Harry Longabaugh[12]

Sheriff Ryan arrived on June 19th and took official possession of the prisoner.[13] The road that ran past the N Bar

line camp was the old stage road between Miles City, Montana, and Deadwood, South Dakota. This time, Ryan and Harry took the stage. A local newspaper reported that "Longabaugh was securely shackled and handcuffed, the shackles being made of steel and riveted with steel rivets, and as they got aboard Ryan informed the kid that he was going to land him or his scalp in Sundance jail. The kid gave him fair warning that he intended to escape and told him to watch him but not to be too rough on him."[14]

They arrived in Sundance, Wyoming, on June 22nd, and Harry was placed in the new jail behind the courthouse, held on grand larceny charges. Court records show that Harry gave his home state as Pennsylvania, his occupation as cowboy, his height as six feet, and his age as twenty-six. However, Harry was only twenty. It seems that the court clerk wrote a very sloppy and often misread zero. The records further indicate that he had no living parents. His mother, Annie, had indeed died in May 1887, but his father, Josiah, was still alive.[15]

CHAPTER 8

The "Kid" Gets a New Name

True to his word, Harry continued his attempts to escape while awaiting trial. He and a fellow inmate named William McArthur managed to remove a bolt from the hinge of their cell door, but it was discovered before an escape could be made.[1] Harry waited impatiently for the court's fall term to begin. On August 3, 1887, he was indicted on three counts of grand larceny:

> *True Bill # 33—Indictment for Grand Larceny. One horse of the value of Eighty Dollars ($80.00) of the personal goods and Chattels of Alonzo Craven then and there being found, then and there feloniously did steal, take and carry away, ride away, drive away and lead away contrary to the form of the Statute in such case made and provided and against the peace and dignity of the Territory of Wyoming.*
>
> *True Bill # 34—Indictment for Grand Larceny.* [The details and description are currently missing.]
>
> *True Bill # 44—Indictment for Grand Larceny. One Revolver of the value of thirty Dollars of the personal goods and Chattels of James Widner, then and there feloniously, did steal, take and carry away contrary to the form of the*

*Statute in such case made and provided and against the
peace and dignity of the Territory of Wyoming.*[2]

The prosecuting attorney in the case was Benjamin F. Fowler,
who later became a U.S. attorney for Wyoming from 1890 to
1894 and the state attorney general from 1895 to 1898. On
August 4th, Judge William L. Maginnis determined that Harry
could not afford an attorney and appointed Joseph Stotts to
represent him. Stotts, a Republican, was later elected to the
state legislature.

On August 5th, Harry originally pleaded not guilty. However, Stotts convinced him to plead guilty to horse stealing,
indictment no. 33, in exchange for the other two indictments
being dropped. A transcript of his court appearance states,
"The defendant Harry Longabaugh was this day again brought
before the court, and having been asked by the court if he
had anything to say why judgement and sentence should not
be pronounced against him upon the plea of guilty in this
cause says he has nothing to say; the court thereupon pronounced sentence upon said plea as follows: the sentence of
the court is that you HARRY LONGABAUGH be confined
in the place designated by the penitentiary commissioner of
the Territory of Wyoming as a penitentiary for the term of
eighteen months at hard labor."[3] However, because of his
age, he was confined to the county jail in Sundance rather
than the penitentiary at Laramie, Wyoming.

According to Crook County Court records, the court-
appointed public defender Stotts was granted $25 for each
of the three indictments, and Judge Maginnis earned $10.95
in fees from the Territory of Wyoming.[4] By the time Harry
was released, it had also cost the Territory over $350 in board
and clothing expense to keep him in jail.

Harry was not yet convinced that he was in jail to stay.
On May 1, 1888, he and a fellow prisoner assaulted the jailor
in an attempt to escape. The *Sundance Gazette* reported: "Just

Governor Moonlight's Pardon, Secretary of State Record of Pardons, Vol. 1, p. 124. Wyoming State Archives, Department of State Parks and Cultural Resources.

before 6 o'clock, as Jailor Daley was taking supper to the prisoners in the county jail, he was suddenly assaulted in the hallway by Jim O'Connor and Harry Longabaugh, two of the prisoners who had effected their escape from the cells. Mr. Daley grappled Longabaugh (the "kid") and succeeded in overpowering him and returned him to his cell. . . . Longabaugh, or "the kid" is the slippery cuss who gave Sheriff Ryan so much trouble, while bringing him to this place from Miles City. He is serving out a sentence of 18 months for stealing a horse on Crow creek two years ago."[5] O'Connor's attempt succeeded, but only temporarily.

In spite of Harry's escape attempts, on January 22, 1889, H. A. Alden, then Crook County prosecutor, wrote to Governor Thomas Moonlight and to Colin Hunter, the secretary of the Board of the Prison Commission, and asked for a pardon for Harry. The letter to Hunter said, "We have forwarded to the Governor a petition for the pardon of Harry Longabaugh whose term will expire on the 5th of February. I should have sent it to you but fearing that you might be away from home and not get it in time I forwarded it directly to him. The Sheriff tells me that you will assist in obtaining a pardon so that the boy may be restored to his civil rights."[6]

On February 4th, just one day before his scheduled release, Harry was granted a full pardon by the governor. "He is still under 21 years of age, and his behavior has been good since confinement, showing an earnest desire to reform. . . . Therefore, I do hereby grant unto Harry Longabaugh a full and complete pardon"[7] However, because of the short time between the signed pardon and his release, it is not known whether Harry ever learned of his pardon.

On February 8, 1889, The *Sundance Gazette* wrote, "The term of 'Kid' Longabaugh expired on Tuesday morning, and the young man at once hired himself to the Hills, taking the coach for Deadwood."[8] But that was not to be the last that the town of Sundance heard of young Harry.

According to the *Sundance Gazette*, Buck Hanby, a cowboy from nearby Newcastle, Wyoming, was wanted for murder by authorities in Greeley County, Kansas.[9] He had recently returned from Nebraska, where he had been exonerated of another murder indictment. On May 17, 1889, Sheriff E. B. Armstrong and Deputy Sheriff James Swisher of Crook County located Hanby in a dugout on Oil Creek, about thirty-five miles south of Sundance, with three other young men, including Harry Longabaugh. When Hanby was ordered to

Street scene, Sundance, Wyoming, circa 1900. Wyoming State Archives, Department of State Parks and Cultural Resources, Sub Neg 1020.

give himself up, he reached for his gun and was killed by Swisher and Armstrong. On May 18th, Swisher swore out a complaint against Harry, because he feared retaliation for Hanby's killing. The warrant was filed on May 24th, and the paperwork indicates that Sheriff J. W. Rogers actually arrested Harry. However, there is no record that the case was ever heard; presumably, Harry escaped or skipped bail.[10]

Harry Alonzo Longabaugh had made the final transition to outlaw. He was now known as the Sundance Kid.

CHAPTER 9

Telluride Bank Robbery

The *Rocky Mountain News* headlined "The robbery of the San Miguel Valley Bank of Telluride on Monday by four daring cowboys." It reported that "the four rode over to the bank, and leaving their horses in charge of one of the number, two remained on the sidewalk and the fourth entered the bank."[1] The first news account actually started an ongoing controversy—did three or four men rob the bank?

The Sundance Kid's cousin, George Longenbaugh, still ranched in Cortez, Colorado, about seventy-five miles from Telluride when the bank was held up by Tom McCarty, Matt Warner, Butch Cassidy, and a possible fourth man. Although the fourth man is often disputed, the Longenbaugh family to this day believes that Sundance was involved with the robbery.

Historian Pearl Baker quoted a local witness named Roy Dickerson, who said, "There were four of the fellows that had robbed the bank at Telluride."[2] Outlaw Tom McCarty, in later years, described the robbery in his autobiography, indicated, "two of my partners," which implied that he had more than two partners.

In answer to a letter from the Longenbaugh family, C. M. Engel, a local historian, did not deny Sundance's participation. Instead, Engel wrote, "Robbed June 10 [*sic*], 1889 by

Butch Cassidy and his gang. Butch and his cohorts were known as 'the wild bunch'. . . . records are confusing and do not always agree. . . . "[3] After Sundance left Wyoming, his whereabouts are unknown; therefore, he may very well have held horses for the robbery.

Why the bank in Telluride? For one thing, large quantities of gold ore were taken out of the Telluride mines. Also, Butch Cassidy and Matt Warner had worked for a local rancher named Harry B. Adsit, and they knew the area well. Matt and Tom McCarty were brothers-in-law, and they had recently invited Butch to join them in a horse racing venture.[4] When the racing business slowed and ranch work became tiresome, the trio decided the San Miguel Valley Bank seemed just the place to make a raid; so they warned town marshal Jim Clark to conveniently absent himself for a day or two. (Clark later bragged about receiving a $2,200 payoff to be out of town.)

On the morning of June 24, 1889, as county clerk Charles Painter left the bank, Butch, Tom, and Matt rode up in front of it on Main Street. The teller, C. Hyde, was alone behind the counter counting a pile of cash in front of him. Tom stayed outside with the horses while Butch and Matt went inside. Matt covered Hyde while Butch jumped over the counter, filled his sack with the loose money, and collected the cash from inside the vault as well. Estimates vary from $10,500 to $30,000, but most newspaper accounts at the time said the cash taken totaled about $20,700.

As the thieves raced out of town, they unexpectedly rode past Adsit, who instantly recognized his ex-employees, Butch and Matt. They were now outlaws on the run, without question. They stayed well ahead of the pursuing posse by means of horse relays that they had set up ahead of time on a well-scouted escape route. Many names have been suggested as horse relay holders, including Sundance, 'Kid' Madden, Bert Charter, and Dan Parker, Butch's younger brother. All these men were future outlaws with a connection to the Cortez and Telluride area.

Robert LeRoy Parker, alias Butch Cassidy, circa 1893

Butch, Matt, and Tom made a successful getaway, headed into Wyoming, and split the proceeds equally. The Longenbaugh family no longer heard from Sundance, but they maintain to this day that he was involved in the Telluride bank robbery.

CHAPTER 10

A Cowboy in Calgary

When Sundance hired on in 1886 with the Suffolk Cattle Company near Newcastle, Wyoming, the neighboring spread was Morton Frewen's 76 Ranch. This ranch was the preferred vacation spot for writer Owen Wister, who years later wrote *The Virginian*. The manager of the 76 during this time was Fred W. Hesse, who a few years later went on to become quite well-known during the Johnson County Cattle War.

Working for Fred Hesse at Frewen's ranch was a young cowboy from Virginia named Cyril Everett "Ebb" Johnson; Ebb and Sundance had developed a close friendship.[1] Ebb often claimed to be the model for the Virginian's character; maybe Sundance also had some influence on the outlaw Trampas in Wister's writing.

About the time that Sundance was sentenced to jail in 1887, Ebb headed north "in the night, on a fast horse," according to his descendants. He soon found a job as foreman of the Bar U Ranch near the town of High River, just south of Calgary. The neighboring ranch was Frewen's Canadian range, the 76 ranch, later called the Midway Ranch.

In the fall of 1889, Sundance drifted north to Canada, where he hoped to have a clean start. He soon arrived at the Bar U in need of work, and Johnson immediately hired him as a horse breaker. The year 1890 was one of the best years ever for the Bar U, which carried 10,410 cattle and 832 horses on its books. So, hiring Sundance, an experienced horse breaker, was a good management decision, as well as a gesture of good friendship.

Sundance was well-liked by his new coworkers and friends. They considered him "good looking, charming, and fearing neither man nor devil."[2] He was further described as "a quiet young cowhand and a good rider." One friend, Fred Ings, from the 76 Ranch, wrote in his memoirs that Sundance was "a thoroughly likeable fellow . . . a general favorite . . . a splendid rider and a top notch cow hand." Ings also mentioned that he suspected Sundance was evading the law in the States but that while in Calgary he was a "decent fine fellow who could not have been better behaved."[3]

In his memoirs, Ings also told of the time that Sundance's expertise probably saved both their lives. They had been riding herd one night during a late fall roundup when a surprise blizzard blew up in a blinding whiteness. It was bitter cold, no relief shift arrived, and they were exhausted. Sundance rode back along the herd until he found Ings and suggested that their best hope lay in giving their horses their heads to see if they could make it back to camp. By the time they finally arrived in camp the next day, the horses had fallen a dozen times into the deep snow; but they were both alive. It took the roundup crew two days to find all the cattle again in the blowing drifts.

On April 6, 1891, in district no. 197 of High River, the Canadian government census enumerated seventeen residents at the Bar U Ranch, among them, "Henry [sic] Longabough, age 25, birthplace USA, occupation horse breaker." Ebb Johnson was also listed as ranch foreman.[4]

Another ranch hand at the Bar U was Herb Millar, a cowboy who clearly did not like Sundance. On August 7, 1891, Sundance was arrested for cruelty to animals by the North

The Bar U Ranch in High River, Canada. Glenbow Archives, NA-466-12.

Ebb Johnson. Glenbow Archives, NA-2924-12.

Grand Central Hotel Saloon, Calgary, Canada. Glenbow Archives, NA-298-3.

West Mounted Police in response to Millar's claim of seeing a small hacksaw hidden between Sundance's saddle and horse blanket. However, the charges were immediately dismissed on the same day they were recorded. Superintendent J. H. McIllree and Inspector A. R. Cuthbert decided not to refile any charges.

The charges were apparently considered groundless, because Sundance remained in the employ of the Bar U Ranch. (Millar was also kept on, eventually retiring as manager after fifty-two years with the Bar U.) Sundance's friendship with foreman Ebb Johnson also continued. On November 18, 1891, Johnson married his sweetheart, Mary Eleanor Bigland, in the Knox Presbyterian Church in the center of Calgary. Ebb asked Sundance to stand up for him as the best man in the wedding.[5]

A particular favorite winter pastime at the ranch was a good game of cribbage. It filled many long and cold hours for the Bar U ranch hands. The regulars, including Sundance and Ebb, each carved their names into the ranch set.

Early in 1892, Sundance left the Bar U Ranch and went into partnership with Frank Hamilton at the Grand Central Hotel Saloon in the city of Calgary. Hamilton was considered to be a hothead; in fact, he had already run off a few previous business partners.

The partnership between Sundance and Hamilton was also short-lived. They argued over payment for a horse that Hamilton had apparently bought from Sundance. Their fight came close to gunfire when Sundance drew down on Hamilton and demanded the $100 he was owed. With the debt paid and the partnership dissolved, Sundance took off south again for the States.

But Sundance left many good friends back in Calgary. They would occasionally hear of his crimes across the border and, as Ings later wrote, "We all felt sorry when he left and got in bad again across the line."[6] It wasn't long before he "got in bad again."

CHAPTER 11

Train Robbery in Malta

As the cold winter of 1892 set in, Sundance sought warmth, food, and drink in Alex Black's Saloon in Malta, Montana, with friends Bill Madden and Harry Bass.[1] They joined the large number of cowboys who had been laid off for the winter and who now hung around town to pass the time of day. Sundance previously knew Bill Madden from Cortez, Colorado, but Harry Bass was apparently a new acquaintance. Bored, broke, and probably a little drunk, the three cowboys decided to add a little excitement and some easy money to their lives.

A train robbery that night seemed just the thing to do. One member of the trio rode about a mile west of town and built a bonfire near the tracks. He sat by the warm fire guarding the escape horses he had brought with him and waiting for his partners to arrive by train.

At 3 A.M. on Tuesday, November 29, 1892, the Great Northern westbound express no. 23 out of St. Paul, Minnesota, made its regular mail and water stop at Malta. The other two cowboys boarded the blind baggage car while the train took on water. As the train began to pick up speed again, they slipped over the coal tender, crept onto the engine, and ordered the engineer to stop near the fire about a mile

54

ahead. The third thief was still tending the fire and holding the horses.

Once the train stopped again, mail clerk Rawlins was ordered to open the mail car, but nothing of value was found there. Two of the thieves then headed for the express car while the third outlaw guarded Rawlins, conductor Bywater, and the train's fireman and brakeman. At the express car, messenger Jerry Hauert was ordered to open the safes, but he replied that he did not have the combination for the larger through safe. The smaller safe, however, held a check for $46.28, another check for $6.80, a small package worth 30 cents, and a second package valued at $10.42—for a grand total of $63.80. One newspaper later reported that $25,000 was missed by the obviously amateur thieves, but that was denied by the railroad. Another newspaper pointed out that the inexperienced outlaws apparently never considered the fact that the express train had left St. Paul on a Sunday, not a banking business day.

Although frustrated with the small amount they found, the robbers toasted the crew with a drink and escaped off into the night. Foolishly, they returned to Malta. The train continued on its regular route, stopping only to telegraph the news of the holdup. "Express car No. 23 entered by robbers just west of Malta. Little of value taken. Nothing done to molest passengers."[2] The express company offered a $500 reward for each of the outlaws, and the governor of Montana offered to match the reward. A local newspaper pointed out that the rewards offered were worth more than the outlaws had stolen, but the railroads wanted to send a clear message that they would not tolerate train robbers.

The first posse did not arrive in Malta until December 1st. It included W. Black, detective for the Great Northern Railroad, Sheriff Hamilton of Cascade County, Sheriff B. F. O'Neal of Choteau County, Undersheriff Matthews, and Harry Lund. When the posse arrived in town, they stopped for a shot of

Malta, Montana, showing railroad round house and Malta Mercantile Company, no date. Photographer unidentified. Montana Historical Society, Helena, Montana, 949-174.

courage, coincidentally in the same saloon where Sundance, Madden, and Bass were once again drinking. The *Great Falls Tribune* reported what happened. "Inside the building there were a number of men who, when they saw them coming, quickly grasped their Winchesters and began throwing cartridges into the magazines. 'Guess you —— of —— of deputy sheriffs are after someone, ain't you?' said one of the gang. 'Well, come right along. We'll make it interesting for you.' The officers saw they were powerless. The men were undoubtedly the robbers, but they had not only been drinking, but were desperate and had resolved not to be captured. . . . So, the Glasgow posse retired."[3]

Although the outlaws were apparently drunk, the confrontation alerted them to their need to leave Malta immediately. At 10 P.M. Harry Bass and a man named William Hunt were arrested by Detective Black as they saddled their horses outside the saloon of Alex Black (no relation to the detective). At about the same time, Sheriff B. F. O'Neal of Choteau County and Sheriff Hamilton of Cascade County arrested saloonkeeper Black and Sundance as they boarded an eastbound train just leaving the Malta depot. Suspect Bill Madden was not found.

The four arrested men were taken first to Helena, where they were identified by conductor Bywater. They were then taken back to Great Falls, where they were arraigned on December 3rd before U.S. Commissioner Pomeroy. They were all bound over for trial, with bail set at $300 each; but none of them had any money. Sundance was held as J. E. Ebaugh, alias J. E. Thibadoe, the names he gave at his arrest.

Two days later, on December 5th, Bill Madden was arrested in Malta and taken to Fort Benton, where he too was held over for trial. Madden was taken to Fort Benton rather than Great Falls because the authorities belatedly realized that the holdup had actually occurred in Choteau County, rather than Dawson County as originally believed. This confusion was later blamed on the lack of a proper surveying of the county line.

Once in Fort Benton, Madden was lodged in the town's new jail—each cell just a 4 x 8 x 6 foot steel cage within the log jailhouse. When the town received the new, mail-ordered jail, they were not prepared for the jigsaw puzzle to be put together. It took them nearly a year to figure out how best to build and secure the bars. A solid metal plate floor and ceiling were eventually riveted into the log facility, with the one-inch steel bars creating three cagelike cells and a 3 x 12 foot exercise hallway.[4]

Under questioning, Madden confessed to his part in the robbery and implicated Bass and a man Madden identified as *Lounghbo*. Meanwhile, on December 8th, a trial was held for the four outlaws still jailed in Great Falls. After hearing testimony concerning the robbery, prosecution witness A. J. Shore unexpectedly made a motion "that the prisoners be discharged for the reason that nothing had been adduced to show that they were guilty of the charge proferred [*sic*] against them."[5] All four prisoners were immediately released.

Hunt and Sundance quickly left town, but Alex Black stopped to toast his good fortune with a drink at the local saloon, where he proclaimed his innocence to anyone who would listen. Harry Bass was immediately re-arrested at the courthouse steps on charges of burglary, based upon Madden's confession and implication. The authorities who released Sundance apparently had not realized that he was, in fact, *Lounghbo*, the second man implicated by Madden.

Bass was taken to Fort Benton, where he was placed in a cell adjoining Madden's. Sheriff O'Neal, detectives Black and Kilgore of the Great Northern, and railroad superintendent G. C. Gates attempted to track Sundance, to no avail. They returned to Great Falls and sent out the following wanted notice:

$ 500 REWARD

The above reward will be paid by the Great Northern Express company for the arrest and detention of Harry Lounghbo [*sic*], who in company with others held up and robbed the west bound train on the Great Northern Railway, near Malta, Montana, on the morning of November 29th, 1892.

Description—Height, 5 feet 11 inches. Dark complexion, short dark moustache, dark hair, Age, about 25 years. Slender and erect, with slight stoop in head and shoulders. Short upper lip, exposing teeth when talking. Teeth white and clean with small dark spot on upper front tooth to right of center. Wore a medium size black soft hat. Dark double breasted sack coat. Dark close-fitting pants with blue overalls. When last seen was riding bay horse branded Half Circle Cross on left shoulder.[6]

Judge Dudley Dubose, of the Tenth Judicial District, in Fort Benton, heard the case of Bill Madden and Harry Bass, who were charged with "Burglary in the Night Time" in connection with the Malta train robbery. Both men pleaded guilty and were immediately sentenced. Sundance, however, was never recaptured or tried for the Malta train robbery.

Madden, who had confessed and implicated Bass and Sundance, received eight years in the state penitentiary; Bass was sentenced to ten years, also in the state system. On Christmas morning, 1892, Madden and Bass were received at the Deer Lodge Penitentiary. Prison records indicate that Bass received a pardon and early release on January 1, 1897; he disappeared from record. Madden was released January 19, 1898, with time off for good behavior; he moved to Oregon City, Oregon, where he was watched by the Pinkertons for some time. With the Southern Pacific Railroad robbery at nearby Walkers, Oregon, they opened a file on him and gave him the cipher *Wolf*.[7]

For about three years, Sundance managed to remain on the right side of the law. He found occasional work at a number of Montana ranches, including the R L, the Circle Bar, and the N Bar. He was also reported to be in the Hole in the Wall area of Johnson County, Wyoming, with his friends Harvey Logan and Flatnose George Currie.

By the summer of 1895, he had hired on again with the N Bar N Ranch.[8] The roster of ranch hands was made at the time that the ranch was again expanding and moving their headquarters to Wolf Point, Montana. Besides Sundance, there were a number of other employees who would become well-known in the future. Listed as cowboys on the N Bar N Ranch were the now famous painter Charlie Russell, outlaw Harvey Logan, and rustler Dutch Henry Ieuch. Sundance certainly had an interesting mix of co-workers.

CHAPTER 12

The Little Snake River Valley

The small ranch towns of Baggs, Dixon, and Savery, Wyoming, along the Little Snake River, were home to Harry Alonzo for about two years. Sundance began using the alias Alonzo in an effort to have a clean start. He was at first a horse breaker for the Beeler Ranch and then a general ranch hand and wrangler for Albert R. Reader at the Stone Wall Ranch. He was considered a good ranch hand and was well liked by the people in the valley.[1] In an interview, Jean Beeler Russell recalled that her older brothers spoke highly of Sundance and of his ability with horses. She further stated that Sundance was "quiet and soft-spoken, a very agreeable person . . . congenial."[2]

Among his friends was Oliver St. Louis, a clerk in Robert McIntosh's store in nearby Slater, Colorado. St. Louis remembered, "He used to go to dances up there [at Reader's] . . . he was a straight man. . . . he was one of the strongest men . . . used to wrestle together and all I could do to throw him."[3]

Next to the Reader ranch in Savery was the Gooldy ranch. John F. Gooldy, who later wrote his memoirs, recalled, "I knew Harry Longabaugh, robber and pal of Butch Cassidy. . . . he went by the name of Harry Alonzo when I knew him. He was a cowboy for A. R. Reader. . . . rode mean horses, and could

Reader's Ranch Barn. Museum of Northwest Colorado.

ride about any horse anyone else could ride. He behaved himself pretty well."[4]

Across the road from the Reader Ranch, Frank Kelsey
owned a small haying operation. He and Sundance developed
a tight friendship, and Sundance occasionally worked with
him. These men from the Little Snake were all steadfast
friends who remained loyal to Sundance even in later years.

According to Gooldy's memoirs, Sundance once worked
for the Ora Haley Ranch, also known as the Two Bar.[5] Haley's
Two Bar was a driving force in the attempt by area big ranchers
to rid Brown's Park of rustlers and sheep. But Sundance
undoubtedly disapproved of Haley's big-handed methods.
His defiance seemed to grow stronger over the years, as it
did also with his socialist-leaning brothers in Pennsylvania
and California.

Eventually, Sundance's past caught up with him. Gooldy
mentions an arrest by Deputy Sheriff "Big" Perkins that may
have been the result of a confrontation with roundup boss

Ed Wren. While under arrest and seated in a wagon, Sundance hit Perkins in the face with his handcuffed fists, which prompted Perkins to say that Sundance obviously had experience wearing handcuffs. As a result of the incident, Wren purchased a gun to protect himself, and Perkins began checking into Harry Alonzo.[6] Soon, the Pinkertons were asking around the valley for information about Harry Alonzo Longabaugh, alias the Sundance Kid.

But Sundance was not the only one being checked into by the Pinkertons. Many honest and hard-working ranchers ended up being listed in dossiers that the agency began collecting. Acquaintances of Harry Alonzo were immediately suspect, often just because of their friendship. Their names also began to appear in Pinkerton Agency cipher lists. Charles F. Tucker, a rancher friend from Dixon, was given the cipher *Shingle*; Robert McIntosh, the postmaster and storekeeper, was *Crow*; Jim Ferguson, a rancher from Battle Mountain, was *Buzzard*; Jim Hansen, a horse breeder and rancher, was *Socks*; Bert Charter, a ranch hand from Reader's Ranch, was *Ostrich*; and Jack Ryan, a Baggs saloonkeeper, was *Basket*.[7]

The Pinkertons also developed local informants, and their most important and vocal informant was Charlie Ayers of Dixon, Wyoming. Ayers, once the foreman for Ora Haley's Two Bar, was a local rancher and a Wyoming Stock Association inspector; his Pinkerton cipher name was *Stamp*. The first full description of Sundance provided to the Pinkertons came from Ayers in October 1900. That description eventually became part of every Wild Bunch wanted poster the Agency released.[8]

> *32–5 ft 10. 175–Med. Comp. firm expression in face, German descent Combs his hair Pompadour, it will not lay smooth– erect, but carries his head down not showing his eyes. eyes Blue or gray. Bowlegged–walks with feet far apart. Carries*

arms straight by his side. fingers closed, thumbs sticking straight out. eats Ralston [breakfast] *food, asks for it, and discusses its merits he uses knife & fork awkwardly very quiet, cowboy. good Rider, marks his clothes "H L" with worsted thread–had catarrh badly*[9]

Ayers was not the only Pinkerton informant from the Little Snake River Valley who knew Sundance well. Emmet Leahy, who once ran a small store in Dixon and was known as *Wax* on the cipher list, likely verified Ayers' report. But, Sundance had trusted Leahy as a good friend. In fact, before Sundance left the States for Argentina, he gave one of his rifles to Leahy as a gift.[10]

Harry Alonzo's law-abiding life along the Little Snake was also a matter of public record. On January 9, 1897, the newspaper from neighboring Craig, Colorado, noted that "Harry Alonzo and Bert Charter went to the lower Snake river last Monday to establish a winter camp and look after the cattle of the Reader company till spring."[11] Then a week later, the newspaper noted, "Reader's outfit left last Monday for the lower country for the winter. Bert Charter, Harry Alonzo, and Mr. Fillbrick were with the horses."[12] Coincidentally, Reader Cabin Draw, the location of Reader's winter camp, bordered the Powder Springs hideout.

CHAPTER 13

Belle Fourche Bank Robbery

Belle Fourche, French for *beautiful fork,* was named for the meeting of South Dakota's Belle Fourche and Redwater rivers. It was a busy cattletown on the railroad, located about fifty miles northeast of Sundance, Wyoming, and only a dozen miles from the Three V Ranch, an area well known to Sundance.

On September 25, 1895, a fire swept through Belle Fourche, destroying much of the town. However, the townspeople banded together and rebuilt the center of town in time to host a weekend reunion of Civil War soldiers and sailors beginning June 24, 1897.[1] The town leaders hoped that the reunion festivities would bring in extra money to help defray the expenses of rebuilding.

Meanwhile, a gang of outlaws led by Flatnose George Currie had also heard about the festivities and decided to rob the Butte County Bank, located on the corner of Sixth and State streets in the center of town. The gang believed that the extra men in town would give them cover, and the extra money being spent might just as well fill their pockets as the town's coffers.

Although often included in the list of outlaws, Sundance was not with the gang, as will be seen. The five outlaws—Currie, Tom O'Day, Walt Punteney, and brothers Harvey and

Butte County Bank, Belle Fourche, S.D. Courtesy Doug Engbretson.

Lonnie Logan—camped just east of town while the celebration was being held. On Monday morning, June 28th, O'Day was sent into town to survey the scene around the bank. Instead of reporting back to camp, he joined some revelers in Bruce Sebastian's Saloon, where he purchased two quarts and a pint bottle of Old Crow whiskey. He imbibed and promptly forgot his assigned task. Although the drunken O'Day did not return to camp, the outlaws decided to go ahead—after all, the bank would be bursting its rafters with extra cash from the weekend activities.

About 10 o'clock in the morning, the other four outlaws rode into town, hitched their horses near the side entrance of the bank, and entered through the front door. They encountered seven men already in the bank and ordered them to hold up their hands. Besides head cashier Arthur H. Marble and his assistant S. W. Harry Tichnor, there were five customers in the lobby—J. H. Chapman, C. A. Dana, the local Methodist minister Dr. E. E. Clough, E. M. Mitchell, and Sam Arnold, who was preparing to deposit $97, including a check for $2.50.

From across the street, hardware store owner Alanson Giles happened to look out his window just in time to see the men in the bank raise their hands into the air. About the same time, O'Day apparently sobered enough to realize his tardiness, exited the saloon, and headed up the street towards the bank. Giles stepped outside to take a closer look at the bank but was chased back inside when O'Day started shooting at him.

The shots not only warned the outlaws of impending trouble but also alerted the townspeople. One of the outlaws grabbed Arnold's $97 as they all ran out the front door. Their anticipated big haul reportedly sat untouched—gold and silver coins were in a teller's tray within easy reach behind the counter.

Mr. Marble grabbed a revolver hidden under the counter and snapped off a couple of rounds at the retreating outlaws. City Marshal Lee Brooks later commented cynically, "When I got there Mr. Marble was shooting, but the robbers were no where in sight."[2] In the tumult, O'Day's untethered horse ran off without him and followed the escaping thieves down Sixth Street, over the railroad tracks, and up Sundance Hill, where the riderless horse was shot by another local, Frank Bennett.

O'Day, in the meantime, jumped on a nearby mule in an attempt to escape, but the mule proved to be too stubborn. He then ran to an outhouse between Sebastian's Saloon and the *Times* printing office in the Andre Building to dispose of his gun. The town butcher, Rusaw Bowman, suspected O'Day's intention and stopped him as he exited the outhouse. The outhouse was overturned and a gun was retrieved with a rake. O'Day's pockets were searched, and gun cartridges were found along with a pint of whiskey and $392.50.

The town had a small problem—on the first night of the celebration, a drunk trying to stay warm had accidentally started a fire that burned down the new jail. With no jail,

Tom O'Day, October 1, 1897. Adams Museum, Deadwood, S.D., 71-147.

Marshal Brooks needed a secure place to confine O'Day.
Ironically, he was placed overnight in the same bank vault that
the gang had just tried to rob. The next day, he was trans-
ferred to the Lawrence County jail in nearby Deadwood, South
Dakota. Once in Deadwood, O'Day hired lawyer W. O. Temple
as his defense attorney.

In the meantime, the other four outlaws headed southwest
and made a clean escape. As they crossed into Wyoming, the

gang split up, and Currie and Lonnie Logan headed for the Hole in the Wall headquarters of Currie's gang of rustlers. Punteney and Harvey Logan turned toward Powder Springs, where Sundance happened to be working at Reader Cabin Draw.

For years, the Pinkertons and outlaw historians have included Sundance in a list of suspected thieves in the Belle Fourche robbery. After all, he knew the area well, and the owners of the bank were John Clay and Robert Robinson, who had been the manager and trail boss of the Three V Ranch at the time of Sundance's 1887 arrest in Sundance, Wyoming. Retribution was once believed to have been a major cause for the robbery; however, a letter written by David Gillespie, Sundance's friend from the Little Snake River Valley, provides proof that Sundance was still in Wyoming working for Al Reader at the time of the robbery. In a letter dated October 12, 1897, David wrote to his mother back home in Illinois.

My dear mother—I can't write more than just a few lines. I haven't really time . . . . I came very near going to Deadwood, South Dakota for a few days and it is barely possible that I may go yet. A young fellow, a friend of mine who worked for Al Reader up till the middle of July left here near the first of August and went up there, and about the first of the month was arrested on the charge of having been in the bank robbery at that place on June 28. He was here at Slater on June 27 and up at Al's ranch on the 28th so couldn't possibly have taken part in the robbery. He fought the officers when they tried to arrest him and was shot in the arm and had his horse shot from under him. When arrested he didn't think it would amount to much so didn't give his right name as he didn't want it to get into the papers. He and his lawyer both wrote here telling how the matter stood and wanted me and one or two others to go there to identify him and prove that he was on Snake River at the time of the bank holdup. Mr. McIntosh said that he could hardly spare me, and if possible they had better get somebody else to go. Two left here last night so I think everything will be all right. I hope the fellow will get off all right for he is a mightly nice fellow. He is the best broncho rider around the country. . . .

Your aft son D. Gillespie[3]

Sundance was accused of participating in the Belle Fourche robbery because of what happened next at the Powder Springs hideout near Reader Cabin Draw.

CHAPTER 14

Capture and Escape

As Punteney and Logan sat around the evening campfire exchanging stories at the Powder Springs hideout, they were joined by Butch Cassidy and Elzy Lay, who had just made a successful raid on the Castle Gate Mining Company, netting over $7,000. Although Logan and Punteney had not been as successful in Belle Fourche, they were still eager for a little bragging. Sundance joined in the celebration from nearby Reader Cabin Draw.

The gang decided to make a visit to Jack Ryan's Bull Dog Saloon in nearby Baggs, Wyoming.[1] On July 29, 1897, they raced into town, generally hurrahed the main street, and shot the saloon full of holes. However, they joyfully made restitution; they paid Ryan one silver dollar for each bullet hole. One local newspaper wrote, "Nine of Butch Cassidy's Gang spent 3 days on Snake River last week, drinking, gambling, and spending about $800 at Baggs and Dixon. Heard Sheriff was coming and left half hour before, returning to their camp in Sweetwater County (Powder Springs), 40 miles away."[2] Ryan soon closed his Bull Dog Saloon in Baggs and bought Con Quinlin's Saloon on Fifth Street in Rawlins, near the Union Pacific Railroad depot with his newfound wealth.

By August, Sundance decided to leave the employ of A. R. Reader and head north with Harvey Logan and Walt Punteney. Their intention was to rob the bank in Red Lodge, Montana.[3] They contacted the town marshal, Byron St. Clair, and suggested that he leave town for a few days. Instead, on September 18th, St. Clair reported the conversation to Carbon County Sheriff John B. Dunn, who gathered a posse made up of attorney Oscar C. Stone, Constable H. J. Calhoun, and stock detectives J. "Dick" Hicks, W. D. "Lame Billy" Smith, and Billy Mendenhall. It is believed that stock detective Lame Billy Smith was the same man as stock inspector W. Smith, who had been involved in the capture of Sundance at the N Bar Ranch on June 1, 1887.

On Wednesday morning, September 22nd, the outlaw trio stopped in Lavina, a small, sleepy town in south-central Montana. They apparently did not know that they were being followed because they stopped in Lavina for a leisurely round of drinks at H. C. Jolly's Saloon. They paid their bar bill with the $2.50 check stolen from the Butte County Bank of Belle Fourche. The local newspaper reported, "It is the supposition that this was one of the checks stolen from the robbed bank four months ago. . . . these facts of themselves will be sufficient to convince most anybody that the men . . . are the ones who robbed the South Dakota bank."[4] The stop in Lavina brought the posse within forty-five minutes of the outlaws.

After riding out of Lavina, Sundance, Harvey, and Walt started to set up camp for the night at a spring on the Musselshell River, about twenty miles north of town. Harvey was picketing his horse, while Sundance and Punteney were headed to the spring for water when the posse suddenly appeared less than one hundred yards away and Dunn called for their surrender. Sundance and Punteney immediately jumped behind the edge of a small bluff, but Harvey "made a rush for his horse and spring [sic] into the saddle. He then drew his Winchester. . . ."[5]

Following a brief gunfight in which Harvey was shot in the wrist, the trio was captured. According to David Gillespie's letter, Sundance also suffered a slight wound to his arm.[6] The posse noted that "a regular arsenal of arms" was captured with the outlaws. Besides the guns and ammunition, they took possession of seven horses, three saddles, and the bedrolls off two dead horses.

The next day, the posse flagged down the Lewistown-Billings stagecoach to transport the outlaws, who were believed to be the Belle Forche robbers, and rode south to Billings, Montana. They were temporarily housed in a cell in the basement of the courthouse. On Saturday, September 25th, S. W. Ticknor arrived from Belle Fourche to identify the trio; he repeated his identification for Justice of the Peace Alex Fraser on Monday morning.

They proclaimed their innocence and gave the names Frank and Thomas Jones and Charley Frost—Sundance, Walt, and Harvey, respectively. They hired lawyer J. B. Herford to defend them and paid him with their extra horses and gear. But, after hearing Ticknor's testimony, Herford advised them to waive the governor's requisition, a legal formality, and return to South Dakota for trial. The posse members put in a joint claim at that time for the $1,875 reward, $625 for each outlaw.

On September 28th, detectives Hicks and Smith escorted Sundance, Harvey, and Walt on the noon Burlington train to Deadwood, where they soon joined Tom O'Day in the Lawrence County jail. The jail was in an old building, located at the intersection of Washington and Monroe streets in Deadwood's residential section. The jail portion of the building was a twenty-foot-square steel cage, in a thirty-foot-square room. The cage boasted an iron floor and steel bars on the windows containing individual cells and a "bullpen" or open walkway for exercise. The prisoners had access to the bullpen daily, but they were locked into their cells at night; a lever operated by the guards dropped a heavy steel bar across the cell doors.

First Deadwood Jail, 1900. Centennial Archives, Deadwood Public Library, collection of John Korneman, Deadwood, S.D.

At the preliminary hearing two days later, a grand jury indicted the men and placed bail at $10,000 each. Local lawyers Frank McLaughlin and W. O. Temple were assigned to represent the outlaws. Still proclaiming his innocence, Sundance asked his lawyers to contact his employer and friends back in Wyoming as material witnesses for his alibi. David Gillespie noted: "He and his lawyer both wrote here telling how the matter stood and wanted me and one or two others to go there to identify him and prove that he was on Snake River at the time of the bank holdup."[7]

On October 2nd, the outlaws were taken to H. R. Locke's photography studio for mug shots. While Walt and Harvey willingly sat for their pictures, Sundance "acted ugly and would not sit for the picture. After trying for some time the machine was snapped but the picture was caught of the top of his head, he having dropped his face and closed his eyes."[8] A search through Locke's archived pictures found only Logan and Punteney's photos still in existence. According to court records, Sundance asked Al Reader, Mrs. Robert (Mary) McIntosh, Dave Gillespie, Joseph Morgan, Frank Kelsey, Jesse Galloway, and Charles Lambert, all upstanding citizens of the Snake River Valley, to testify on his behalf.[9] Based upon that request and the necessary travel time, Sundance's lawyers asked for, and received, a delay in the trial. Two friends, Galloway and Kelsey, left the valley immediately; but by the time the men from the valley arrived in Deadwood, it was already too late.

About 8:45 P.M., on October 31st, Deputy Sheriff John Mansfield and his wife checked the prisoners while returning home from Sunday evening services. When Mansfield ordered the prisoners to enter their cells so he could throw the lever to bar the doors, they claimed the bar was already thrown, locking them out of the cells.

As Mansfield entered the bullpen area to check, another inmate, William Moore, jumped him and knocked him to the floor. Sundance quickly placed his foot in the cell door to prevent Mrs. Mansfield from slamming it shut while Tom O'Day and Harvey Logan joined Moore in kicking her husband into submission. When Mrs. Mansfield protested, they slapped her, threw her on the cell floor along with her husband, and locked the door with them inside.

The four inmates made their way out the rear kitchen door, through the courtyard gate, and escaped on four horses, previously hidden along with supplies by Lonnie Logan.[10] Moore scaled a fence in the side yard and disappeared into the night; when two horses were later stolen from a local ranch, Moore was suspected. Within an hour, the Mansfields were freed, and Sheriff Plunkett and Deputy James Harris were out searching with a posse of sixty men.

Tom and Walt were recaptured on November 2nd just ten miles away near Spearfish, South Dakota. They had become so cold and hungry after two days on the lam that

Walter Punteney, October 1, 1897. Adams Museum, Deadwood, S.D., 71-146.

they were too weak to steal a farmer's horse to replace their exhausted mounts. The weary outlaws' inability to grab the horse had attracted an audience of laughing locals, and in turn caused the pair's easy arrest by Marshal Dave Craig. Once again, Punteney and O'Day were lodged in the jail in Deadwood.

The following April, Walt Punteney was brought to trial. He was found not guilty for lack of evidence, with the help of the testimony of two friends from Thermopolis, Wyoming, who said that both Punteney and O'Day were in Wyoming on the day before the Belle Fourche robbery. The frustrated prosecutor immediately served papers on Punteney for his part in shooting up the town while fleeing the posse. Walt's plea was self-defense, and the jurors again found him not guilty.

The disgusted prosecutors and angry bank officials refused to waste their time and money again in the prosecution of O'Day, so all charges were dropped. Both outlaws walked out of the Deadwood jail free men. Many years later, Punteney told an acquaintance the details of his participation in the Belle Fourche robbery. Not only did he admit to the holdup but he also claimed that the gang got much more than $97. "Now, I ain't makin' no confessions, understand? But you must agree, that I've got myself a right nice little homestead."[11]

Meanwhile, Sundance and Harvey had made a clean escape. One Pinkerton report placed Sundance back on the Little Snake River Valley during the winter of 1897–98, working for his friend Frank Kelsey, whose ranch was just across the road from the Reader Ranch in Savery, Wyoming.[12]

CHAPTER 15

Two Nevada Robberies

From late 1897 through the spring of 1898, Sundance's whereabouts are uncertain and unverified; but with the shortage of winter work, cowboys often drifted from line camp to ranch, chopping wood in exchange for a warm bed and a hot meal. Some researchers claim that he hid out either in southeastern Arizona or on the W S Ranch in Alma, New Mexico. The Pinkertons believed he wintered in Wyoming.[1]

According to the Pinkertons, with the arrival of spring, he headed for the mining town of Eureka, Nevada, where a distant cousin, Seth Longabaugh, lived. Seth, originally from California, was a barkeeper and a Mason in Eureka, and the Pinkertons believed Sundance visited him quite often over the next two or three years. But all sources agree that, by the summer of 1898, Sundance was in Humboldt County, Nevada.

On July 14, 1898, the Southern Pacific passenger train no. 1, traveling east, arrived on time at the Humboldt Station in Humboldt.[2] The once-beautiful combination hotel, restaurant, and depot was one of the few businesses still thriving in town after the area silver panic all but destroyed the place. In its prime, the depot was an elegant stopover, with its outside fountain and surrounding gardens and shade trees. According to an old advertisement, travelers could enjoy "the best meal on the line; cost 75 cents in coin or $1 paper."

As the train pulled out of the depot at 1:25 A.M., two outlaws boarded the rear of the tender car. A mile up the track, they climbed over the tender and covered engineer Philip Wickland and fireman McDermott with their revolvers. The train was stopped immediately, but the thieves ordered the engineer to pull ahead slowly to a large pile of railroad ties, at milepost no. 3784, where a third outlaw waited with the escape horses.

Unknown to the outlaws, when the train was stopped unexpectedly, the rear brakeman became suspicious and jumped off the train. He raced back to Humboldt and telegraphed the town of Winnemucca, the next major stop along the railroad line. A special train car and posse began to ready under the command of Sheriff Charles McDeid and Deputy Sheriff George Rose.

Meanwhile, the express messenger Hughes was ordered to open the express car door. When he refused, a stick of dynamite was exploded at the rear door in warning, stunning Hughes. At the suggestion of the thieves, Wickland and McDermott then strongly urged that the agent come out before he was blown up along with the train. They also asked him not to come out shooting, fearful that they would be caught in a crossfire. The door was slowly opened, and the outlaws jumped on board.

One of the robbers set a second charge on the top of the safe, and ran from the train yelling for everyone to seek shelter. The dynamite succeeded in blowing open the safe, tearing apart the train roof, and destroying the interior of the express car. The outlaws cleaned out the wrecked safe, taking nearly $26,000 and a few pieces of jewelry.

The three outlaws wrapped their feet in the torn and empty money sacks to disguise their boot prints; politely shook hands with Wickland, McDermott, and Hughes as they told them to pull the train out; and jumped on their horses and escaped toward the north.

The train soon met the special posse car traveling from Winnemucca near Mill City, about ten miles east of the holdup site. Although the outlaws already had a two-hour head start, Sheriff McDeid and his posse decided to scout the robbery site for clues before taking off after the train robbers.

The posse included McDeid, Phil Boyle, Constable Feliz of Lovelock, Deputy Sheriff George Rose, Clarence Sage, and an unnamed Indian tracker. They easily discovered the location of the horses and a bundle containing fourteen more sticks of dynamite.

The posse followed the outlaws' trail, marked with hoof-prints and discarded silver watch cases, but quickly gave up the chase because they lacked supplies and fresh mounts. In view of a $1,000 reward offered for each robber by the railroad and Wells, Fargo Express Company, however, Sheriff McDeid stayed on top of every clue that came his way.

Two men named Shaw and Bowie were soon arrested in Oregon and tried in Winnemucca for the Humboldt train robbery. A third man, Dan "Red" Pipkin, was arrested in Utah but was released to the state of Arizona for an earlier warrant. During the trial, George S. Nixon testified as a hand-writing expert regarding a note the posse found along the escape route, which matched writing samples from Shaw and Bowie.[3] When Shaw and Bowie were acquitted, both the Pinkertons and Nixon were reportedly furious. (The graphologist would later have another chance at testifying against thieves.)

In spite of the earlier arrests, the Pinkertons believed the actual outlaws were Sundance, Harvey Logan, and Flatnose George Currie who supposedly were all in the Humboldt area at the time of the Southern Pacific passenger train that summer night.[4]

Drawing of Humboldt Station, Humboldt, Nevada. Nevada Historical Society, Reno, Nev., RR-120.

A year later, the robbery of a small saloon in Elko, Nevada, was blamed on the same trio of men who held up the train in Humboldt. That presumably meant Sundance, Harvey, and Flatnose were the thieves; but this robbery was not their style. It was perpetrated on a small businessman, not on a money-grabbing corporation. In 1899, the Elko newspaper editorialized, "For some time past Elko has been harboring many tough characters."[5]

The Club Saloon, owned by E. M. James Gutridge and located on Railroad Street, was rumored to have a large

amount of cash in the safe. On Monday, April 3, 1899, Gutridge closed up at midnight, shortly after the town constable,
Joe Triplett, left the building. C. B. Nichols, the night bartender,
was at the open safe behind the bar counting the evening
receipts with Gutridge when three masked men came in with
drawn pistols.

Gutridge unsuccessfully hollered for Triplett to return
and was hit on the side of his head in retaliation. While one
outlaw covered the door, another one took Gutridge and
Nichols around to chairs in front of the bar. The third outlaw
then cleaned out the safe, somewhere between $550 and
$3,000, depending upon one's source.

The thieves then warned Gutridge to stay seated and
quiet for two minutes while they backed out of the saloon to
their waiting horses. By the time the alarm was given, the
outlaws had escaped toward Tuscarora, Nevada.

Gutridge immediately suspected three locals named John
Page, J. Cook, and Bart Holbrook; however, when brought
before Justice Morgan, they each had sound alibis and were
consequently freed. Local toughs Frank Bozeman, Joe Stewart,
and John Hunter were then suggested, in part because they
had all left town on the same night as the robbery.

When the Winnemucca, Nevada, bank was held up by
three men eighteen months later, the authorities suspected
that they were the same three who had earlier stopped the
train in Humboldt and robbed the Club Saloon in Elko. Once
again, the Pinkertons listed Sundance, Harvey, and Flatnose
as the bandits, but a saloon robbery was not in character for
Sundance and his criminal partners.

CHAPTER 16

Wilcox Train Robbery

Wilcox Station, Wyoming, no longer exists; however, in 1899 it was a busy railroad town on the Union Pacific Railroad. Originally built as a section house and watering station, the settlement grew at a slower rate than the railroad town of Rock Creek, about ten miles away. Watering stations were necessary for the engines and were usually built about every ten miles. The depot at Rock Creek serviced nearby Fort Fetterman as well as area ranchers, and the depot housed large warehouses that were used by the government as a supply and loading point.[1]

At 2:18 A.M., on June 2, 1899, the Union Pacific Overland Flyer Section no. 1 was flagged down by two men who were waving lanterns at milepost no. 609. It was a rainy Friday morning, and engineer W. R. Jones thought a small wooden bridge up ahead might have washed out overnight. When he brought the train to a screeching halt, the two masked bandits boarded the locomotive and ordered Jones and fireman Dietrick to pull the train ahead to the bridge and stop again.

Dynamite, already tucked under the trestle, was ignited, and Jones was again ordered to pull ahead and be quick about it. When he reacted too slowly for the outlaws, one of them clubbed him with the butt of his Colt revolver. The train barely cleared the bridge when the explosion echoed throughout the countryside.

Although not destroyed, the bridge had suffered enough damage to prevent the second section of train, following about ten minutes behind, from crossing. The passenger cars were uncoupled from the engine, baggage, mail, and express cars; and conductor Storey raced through the passenger cars warning everyone not to interfere. Jones was then ordered to pull two miles farther up the track toward Medicine Bow where four more outlaws were waiting.

Three of the gang herded the trainmen over to the mail car and ordered clerks Robert Lawson and Burt Bruce to open up. When the clerks did not immediately comply, the door to the mail car was blown with more dynamite. Finding little of value, the outlaws next ordered express car messenger Charles Woodcock to open the door on his car. He also refused. Again the outlaws put a match to a stick of dynamite and easily blew the express car door open.

Badly dazed with a concussion, Woodcock was unable to supply the thieves with the combination to the Pacific Express Company safe. Therefore, more dynamite was used to blow it open. However, the second charge proved a bit heavy and succeeded in not only opening the safe but also blowing out the sides and the roof of the express car.

One newspaper account said the outlaws used a total of two hundred pounds of dynamite, all stolen from a nearby railroad work crew. However, the *Saratoga Sun,* of Encampment and Saratoga, Wyoming, reported "the powder was purchased of Gus Jenson & Bro at this place as the packages found near the scene of the robbery were so marked."[2] Yet a third report mentioned that the outlaws needed ten pounds of dynamite just to blow open the safe. A Union Pacific employee, Finley P. Grindley, who happened to be a passenger on the train, reportedly scouted the area and soon found an unused fifty-pound sack of dynamite, hobbled relay horses, and supplies.

Wreckage of car from Wilcox Train Robbery, June 2, 1899. Wyoming State Archives, Department of State Parks and Cultural Resources, Sub Neg 12122.

In just under two hours, the six bandits had gathered unsigned bank notes, cash, nineteen scarf pins, twenty-nine gold-plated cuff button pairs, and four Elgin watches. The initial estimate claimed a total of $30,000 stolen, but in 1904 then Union Pacific superintendent W. L. Park wrote that the railroad had actually lost more than $50,000, some of it in gold.[3]

The outlaws escaped in a northerly direction toward the Hole in the Wall hideout, but they soon split up, with three headed north. The three robbers heading south were followed by Sheriff Swanson out of Rock Springs, Wyoming, and the other posses followed the northerly group. Once the outlaws had left the scene, the railroad crew limped their broken train into Medicine Bow, the next regular stop about twelve miles away, where engineer Jones reported the holdup by telegram just before dawn to Union Pacific headquarters in Omaha, Nebraska.

"First Section No. 1 held up a mile west of Wilcox. Express car blown open, mail car damaged. Safe blown open; contents

Safe blown up during Wilcox Train Robbery, June 2, 1899. Wyoming State Archives, Department of State Parks and Cultural Resources, Sub Neg 9720.

gone . . . we were ordered to pull over bridge just west of Wilcox, and after we passed the bridge the explosion occurred. Can't tell how bad bridge was damaged. No one hurt except Jones; scalp wound, and cut on hand. Jones, Engineer." A second telegram added that "the bent of the bridge was shattered" but that it was repaired enough for trains to pass with caution.[4]

An immediate dispatch was released from railroad head-quarters offering "$1000 reward for each and every one of the train robbers . . . dead or alive." Later, the Pacific Express Company, which owned the safe that was blown open, made a matching offer, as did the United States government. The Union Pacific quickly sent train no. 4—a specially outfitted train kept at the ready in Laramie, Wyoming, containing cars for horses, equipment, food, and men—to the robbery site. This posse train arrived at the site about 9 A.M., just seven hours after the holdup.

The Union Pacific had its own detective force, but the railroad also brought the Burlington Railroad and the Pinkerton Detective Agency into the chase. These professionals joined with the local posses, one of which even employed bloodhounds. Wyoming's Governor DeForest Richards also dispatched Company C of the state militia. Within twenty-four hours of the robbery, nearly one hundred posse members were out chasing the train robbers.

A number of locals were suspected at first, but the professional detectives quickly became focused on members of the Wild Bunch. Although the gang was disguised with masks, their physical descriptions convinced the authorities that known outlaws were involved. One man was *"about 31 or 32 years of age . . . 5' 9" . . . 185 . . . blue eyes . . . peculiar nose, flattened at bridge."* That was a definite match for Flatnose George Currie. *"Two men looked like brothers . . . 5' 7" and 5' 5" . . . about 28 and 30 . . . very dark complexion . . . ¼ Cherokee . . . dark hair & eyes."* This could easily describe Harvey Logan and his brother Lonnie, who often rode with Flatnose. The other outlaws involved in the holdup were believed to be Sundance; Ben Kilpatrick, alias the Tall Texan; Will Carver; or Bob Lee, a cousin of the Logan brothers.

Butch Cassidy, while likely in on the planning stage, did not participate in the actual Wilcox holdup. On January 19, 1896, he had been granted a pardon by Wyoming Governor

William A. Richards and was released from the penitentiary at Laramie. A condition for Butch's early release was his promise to never again participate in any crimes within the borders of Wyoming, and Butch was a man of his word.

Furthermore, soon after the robbery, Butch ran into William L. Simpson, his one-time neighbor and the lawyer who had orchestrated his pardon. Simpson accused Butch of going back on his word, but Butch denied doing that. Simpson wrote, "The last time I saw [Butch] was immediately after the Wilcox robbery on the Union Pacific, and I met him on the Muddy, between Fort Washakie and Thermopolis, Wyoming, and spent an hour with him. I told him he had been accused of being in the Wilcox robbery, that he had promised Governor Richards, [Judge] Jesse Knight and myself that he was not to turn a trick in Wyoming, and he assured me that while he was on his get-away that he had nothing whatever to do with the Wilcox robbery . . . and I know this to be true."[5]

Apparently, Butch did receive a share of the loot because, a few days after meeting Simpson, Butch traded in a "considerable volume of gold coin" at Tom Skinner's saloon in Thermopolis.[6] Also, the posses following the outlaws' trail noticed that an extra set of tracks had joined those of the escaping outlaws. It was believed they belonged to the gang's strategist and mastermind, Butch Cassidy.

In typical Wild Bunch fashion, the outlaws had set up horse relays along their escape route, in order to outrun the posse. After dividing the money, the gang split up, to better evade their pursuers. Flatnose, Harvey, and Sundance made a brief rest stop at Al Hudspeth's CY Ranch near Horse Ranch, Wyoming, but Hudspeth quickly reported the strangers to authorities in nearby Casper.

A posse led by Sheriff Josiah Hazen of Converse County briefly caught up to the thieves, and a small gunfight broke out in which a couple of its horses were wounded. According to local historian Alfred J. Mokler, Hazen's posse included

Dr. J. F. Leeper, E. T. Payton, Al Hudspeth, J. F. Crawford, Sam Fish, J. B. Bradley, Lee Devine, Tom McDonald, and Charles Haegney.[7] Sundance, Harvey, and Flatnose quickly escaped in a northerly direction.

On June 5th, the group that included Sundance was tracked by Hazen's fourteen-man posse near the junction of Teapot and Castle Creeks. (In later years, this area was renamed Teapot Dome and in the 1920s became infamous in a scandal involving its fraudulent leasing by Secretary of the Interior Albert S. Fall.) The outlaws soon reached Jumbo Water Hole, a well-known landmark in the area, where they rested under a rock ledge.[8]

As the outlaws rested, the posse unknowingly rode right in upon them. A gunfight broke out, ending when Hazen received a mortal wound, reportedly from Harvey Logan's gun. A diary entry in Sheriff Frank Hadsell's private correspondence reads, "(Charles) Woodward says White River Charlie, Jack McKnight, and Hank Boyed alias Longbaugh [sic] killed Hazen."[9] Years later, in South America, Sundance occasionally used the alias Frank Boyd.

The remaining posse members hunkered down, numb with fear. But the thieves had staked their horses in the box canyon to the west. The outlaws' only escape was by foot, up the draw to the northeast, on a path that would lead them to the Hole in the Wall. Sundance, Harvey, and Flatnose managed to sneak away, leaving the posse still in hiding and under cover. Due to the heavy rain, the two creeks in the area had reached flood stage. As the outlaws were caught in a rush of water, they had to abandon a portion of the loot. In the 1940s, a small bag of paste jewelry was discovered in the muddy creek bottom by two local boys and was presumed to be jewelry from the Wilcox heist.[10]

Once it became apparent that the outlaws were gone, the posse transported the dying Hazen by wagon to Casper, Wyoming, some of them riding the horses deserted by the outlaws. His body was then placed in a casket and given a ride of honor on the train to Douglas, Wyoming. The newspaper in Rawlins reported, "A short dispatch from Douglas Tuesday night announced the death of Sheriff Joe Hazen of that city from the effects of a wound received in a fight with the robbers on Monday."[11] The posse claimed that the outlaws had managed to outshoot them in part because of a relatively new invention, smokeless gunpowder.

In his book on Powder River history, local rancher J. Elmer Brock claimed that Flatnose, Harvey, and Sundance picked up fresh horses at the Billy Hill ranch near Kaycee, Wyoming, rode through the Brock family ranch, and headed toward EK Mountain.[12] He further stated that the well-known lawman Joe LeFors appeared soon after with a local posse and spent the night on his family's ranch. According to Brock, the posse included the Pinkerton informant Tom Horn, Sheriff Newt Lane of Johnson County, George Munkers, and local officer Brown Parker. When the posse left, they took nearly all the family's food and blankets. Brock concluded, "Isn't it strange that as many outlaws as had been in that place that the first people to commit petty larceny should be a bunch of United States Marshals?"[13]

Brock's comment is of particular interest because it provides insight into the feelings of many local ranchers. Since the rustlers and the outlaws had sided with Wyoming homesteaders against the larger ranch outfits during the earlier Johnson County War, the small ranchers often overlooked the outlaws' questionable behavior.

There were numerous rumors of local residents suspected of supplying the gang with horses, food, and lodging. However, no one was ever indicted or arrested. One posse member was quoted as saying that the bandits would never be caught because they "were aided by powerful friends, there is no doubt."[14] A letter later written to Frank Hadsell by the Pinkertons states, "The train robbers were chased to Powder river

Posse examining remains of Express Car, Wilcox Train Robbery, June 2, 1899. Wyoming State Archives, Department of State Parks and Cultural Resources, Sub Neg 17945.

on foot. Here they fell in with some cattle rustlers, who furnished them with horses and provisions . . . gave Mrs. Nolin a watch. Mr. Nolin, a rustler, had two other watches. . . in part payment for the horses and provisions. The Nolins' live seventy five miles from Buffalo."[15] A short time later, Mrs. Nolin's brother, Joe Gant, was arrested with one of the watches from the Wilcox robbery.

Jack Ryan, the saloonkeeper from Baggs and Rawlins, Wyoming, was specifically suspected of supplying secret railroad information, such as when the larger gold shipments were usually carried.[16] After selling his Bull Dog Saloon in Baggs, Ryan supplemented his income as a brakeman and substitute freight conductor for the Union Pacific Railroad. Then suddenly, on the same day as the Wilcox robbery, Ryan sold his saloon in Rawlins to S. A. Olson and Fred Anderson. According to the Rawlins newspaper, he invested his profits into the Home Ranch Saloon in the newly constructed two-story Cheatum Building.[17]

Two weeks after the robbery, the famous Pinkerton detective Charles A. Siringo began following the gang members and tracing the unsigned bank notes, which soon surfaced in Monticello, Utah; Alma and Mogollon, New Mexico; and Durango, Mancos, and Cortez, Colorado, near the homestead of Sundance's cousin. One of the stolen items was a packet of money described as "incomplete currency, $3400 from U.S. Treasury Department . . . for First National Bank, Portland, Oregon."[18] This package contained currency with known serial numbers and had sustained damaged corners in the explosion, enabling Siringo to follow the paper trail easily. The Pacific Express Company and the U.S. Marshal's office issued memos to agents, bankers, merchants, and others listing the denominations and bank numbers for the package of missing bills. The description included the notation "lower right hand corners all torn diagonally." After following a number of false leads, Siringo was three weeks behind, and he finally lost the trail on the Mississippi River.

Soon after the robbery, the owners of the Curry Brothers Saloon in Harlem, Montana, Lonnie Logan and his cousin Bob Lee, deposited some of the stolen money with their evening receipts; but the bank sent the bills on to Helena because of their torn corners. The serial numbers on the bills were quickly identified as part of the Wilcox loot, and the Pinkertons were immediately notified.

On a tip, Lonnie and Bob sold their share of the saloon and disappeared almost overnight. They headed south to Cripple Creek, Colorado, where they figured to launder the remaining torn bills at the gambling tables. While Bob took up a job dealing faro, Lonnie left town for a brief visit with his aunt and uncle in Dodson, Missouri. But the Pinkertons were just days behind them. On February 28, 1900, Aunt Lizzie's son Bob was taken into custody in Cripple Creek on suspicion of being one of the Wilcox outlaws.

Wilcox train robbery site today

At nearly the same moment, Lonnie noticed men sneaking up on his aunt's farmhouse. Pinkerton agents and Kansas City detectives were attempting to arrest Lonnie for the Wilcox robbery, but Lonnie tried to escape out the back door of the kitchen and into the woods at the rear of the property. The Pinkertons saw him running and shot to kill; Lonnie landed in a snow bank and died instantly. William A. Pinkerton later praised his agents' work.

In a lengthy deposition, given from prison on May 5, 1897, Bob Lee stated that he believed Sundance was the man he knew as Frank Scramble.[19] He stated, "Lonnie Logan had furnished horses for them in Montana after Harvey Logan and Scramble escaped from the Deadwood jail. Scramble is the man who sent the mutilated money to Lonnie Logan. . . . this money was due Lonnie by Scramble for the horses. He [Scramble] sent it to him [Lonnie] from a point near Galveston, Texas some time last summer [1899]." Bob twice repeated the information that Sundance went to Texas following the Wilcox robbery. That statement poses a question: was Sundance there to visit a young woman he had previously known in Texas?

In October 1900, just over a year after the Wilcox robbery, the Union Pacific Railroad rerouted its track to the Southwest. The change, which shortened the stretch of track in Albany County by thirty miles, was part of an ongoing project by the railroad to straighten the path of the tracks. In the course of their project, the Union Pacific bypassed the railroad towns of Rock Creek and Wilcox Station. The new towns, Wilcox and Rock River, never fully made a successful transition.

In return for the inconvenience caused by the track relocation for local ranchers, the Union Pacific Railroad once again blew up the Wilcox bridge, but this time it was to dam up the creek known as Rock Creek, over which the bridge had traveled. That dam now serves as a watering hole for ranches and cattle throughout the area.

CHAPTER 17

They Called Her Etta

David Gillespie, from the Little Snake River Valley, received a photograph of Sundance with a woman, and in the accompanying letter, Sundance identified the woman as being his wife, "a Texas lady he had known previously."[1]

At least two sources—Bob Lee and the Pinkertons—suggested that, after the Wilcox train robbery, Sundance headed for Texas. Presumably, that was when and where he met her. Except for her half-dozen years with Sundance, very little about her is certain.

Her birth name, for instance, is unknown.[2] The Pinkertons list her as Eva, Etta, Rita, and Ethel, as well as Mrs. Longabaugh and Mrs. Place. Their almost exclusive use of the name Etta probably resulted from a typographical error or from a Spanish to English translation error. The name she used exclusively in Argentina was Ethel Place, wife of Harry A. Place, an alias Sundance used at that time.

The explanation for her surname *Place* is relatively simple; it came about through her marriage to Sundance while he was using the alias Harry A. Place. His mother's maiden name was Place. Whether truly wed or in a common-law marriage, they presented themselves as husband and wife. Whoever she was originally, she became Mrs. Ethel Place.

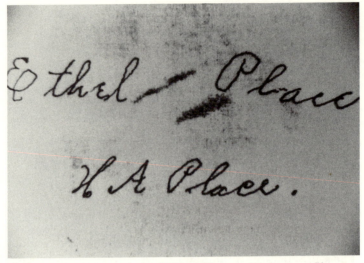

Signatures of Harry A. and Ethel Place in Pinkerton files

Further evidence of her name surfaced when the Pinkertons discovered a register containing both her signature and Sundance's. It clearly reads Ethel Place, and a tracing of her signature is in her Pinkerton files today.

Except for photographs showing her to be strikingly beautiful, the only description we have comes from a visit she and Sundance made in May of 1902 to Dr. Pierce's Invalids Hotel, a private hospital facility in Buffalo, New York. It read: Mrs. Harry A. Place, age 23 or 24, 5 ft f. 110#. Med. Comp Medium dark hair Blue or gray eyes regular features. No marks or blemishes."[3] Presumably, the report was provided to the Pinkertons when it was discovered that Sundance and Ethel had visited the hospital.

A few years later, the Pinkertons expanded that description on their wanted posters: "Mrs. Harry Longabaugh, alias Mrs. Harry A. Place, alias Ethel Place . . . 27 or 28 years old, 5' 4" to 5' 5", 110 to 115 pounds, medium build, medium

Mr. and Mrs. Longabaugh, also known as Harry and Ethel Place, circa 1900

dark hair, which she wears high on top of head in a roll from forehead and medium dark complexion."

Also on the wanted posters was a copy of the portrait she and Sundance had taken together at the DeYoung Photography Studio at 826 Broadway in New York City on February 3, 1901. It was this photograph that had been sent to Sundance's friend David Gillespie in the Little Snake River Valley. According to a Pinkerton memo dated July 29, 1902, "We have ordered copies of a photograph which Longbaugh [*sic*] had taken of himself and the woman . . . said to be his wife and to be from Texas."[4]

Nearly every Pinkerton record about Ethel suggests that she came from Texas. In a letter dated May 12, 1906, William A. Pinkerton asked J. H. Maddox, the chief of police in Fort Worth, to "try to learn through some of your acquaintances in Texas who this woman is and where she came from."[5] Retired Pinkerton agent Frank P. Dimaio wrote to author James D. Horan on June 14, 1949: "She evidently had parents in Texas. . . . My impression is that he may have met her in a house of ill fame . . . but I have no personal knowledge."[6]

It was speculation of Dimaio's that forever identified her as a prostitute; others, however, have suggested that she was a teacher, ranch girl, wife, and mother. Regardless, her background and identity remain a mystery. If Sundance spent time with her after the Wilcox holdup, maybe she really was just a young teacher or ranch girl from Texas; and he may have spent as much as a full year with her before leaving once again for Wyoming.[7] He was expected to participate in another upcoming Union Pacific train robbery.

CHAPTER 18

Tipton Train Robbery

Around the middle of August 1900, Jim Ferguson, one of Sundance's closest friends on the Little Snake River, handed a note to Bill Cruzan, a contact for Wild Bunch members. He was informed : "Harry Alonzo says he cannot be at that place."[1] Cruzan had been in Rawlins, Wyoming, with Harvey Logan helping the gang with logistics for their next holdup. The plan was to stop another Union Pacific train, this time in Tipton, Wyoming. Sundance was originally expected to participate in the upcoming train robbery, but he had decided against it in favor of another holdup.[2]

At least one horse was purchased from Ferguson whose ranch was located in nearby Battle Mountain. It was described as "Brown: star on forehead, snip nose, has pothook right shoulder, white left hind foot inside."[3] After the robbery, when the Pinkertons traced the captured horse back to Ferguson's ranch, they interviewed him at length. He admitted selling the horse to Harvey and told the Pinkertons about the note Sundance had sent to Cruzan, declining to participate.

Sundance's Pinkerton file includes a statement about the Tipton robbery that reads, "In August 1900 Longbaugh [*sic*] agreed to take part in a train robbery on the Union Pacific road with Harvey Logan, but mean while having met Butch

Cassidy he decided to go with Cassidy to Nevada and sent word to Logan by Jim Ferguson he could not keep his appointment."[4] Butch was not interested in the Tipton plan because of his promise to Governor Richards at the time of his pardon; he had given his word not to participate in any Wyoming robberies.

In spite of the note and the Pinkerton interviews of his friends, Sundance is almost always included in the list of suspects for the Tipton train robbery. It is certainly possible that both Butch and Sundance had a part in the planning stages of the holdup; however, the robbery was led by Harvey Logan, along with Ben Kilpatrick, Cruzan, and one or two locals. One Rawlins newspaper claimed that the Tipton robbery was perpetrated by "the same gang as the Wilcox robbery, Butch Cassidy's Gang."[5] It further noted that, "Butch and gang members were seen that summer in the Snake River Valley." A memoir written by Margaret McIntosh Boice, the daughter of Robert McIntosh in Slater, repeated local tradition. "I remember after the Union Pacific train robbery at Tipton, the Authorities felt that the robbers would 'hole-up' on Snake River as two of them were married to local girls."[6]

The Pinkerton detectives further suggested that local ranchers Jim Ferguson and Jim Hansen, and saloonkeeper John Ryan, all of the Little Snake River Valley area, "should be arrested as accessory before and after the fact," based upon their statements.[7] Ryan was believed to have supplied information about currency shipments on the Union Pacific line. The Pinkertons became even more suspicious of Ryan when on December 12, 1900, he optioned to buy the Club Saloon and Gambling Hall in downtown Rawlins.[8] But no warrants were ever issued. Considering the large amount of information that Ryan began to supply the Pinkertons about this time, he may have traded his knowledge for his freedom. In fact, local Sheriff L. G. Davis had recently bragged about planting a mole in the gang, and Ryan fit the picture.[9]

By late August, residents of the small rail town of Tipton had noticed a couple of strangers around town a few days before the robbery. They ate at the small railroad company eating house run by Mr. and Mrs. William Running, according to waitress Lizzie Warren. They were also seen by locals A. Iverson and Joe J. Maloney over two or three days prior to the robbery. The men were apparently casing the area.

On Wednesday, August 29, 1900, about 2:30 A.M., the Union Pacific passenger train no. 3 made its scheduled stop to take on water. The tracks led upgrade a mile or two out of town, so the train left town slowly. As it started westward toward Table Rock, a man was seen racing for the engine.

Engineer Henry Wollenstein soon spotted a fire signal waving the train to a stop next to milepost no. 740.4. The outlaws boarded and ordered conductor E. J. Kerrigan to unhitch the engine, baggage, and express cars from the passenger cars; but Kerrigan insisted on setting the brakes for the first section of cars. He then warned the passengers to keep their heads inside the train windows.

The four masked bandits held Winchesters on the crewmen as the detached cars were moved a short distance away and stopped again. The outlaws then ordered the train messenger to open up the express car. The messenger refused to open the doors until Kerrigan convinced him that dynamite was being readied to blow the doors open anyway. Imagine everyone's surprise when it was Charles Ernest Woodcock, the same messenger who had been injured in the blast in the Wilcox robbery. While Kerrigan's warning had delayed the outlaws, Woodcock had successfully hidden two packages of money from the safe behind a nearby trunk.

Once the train car doors were opened, it took three charges to blow open the safe, as well as the roof, sides, and ends of the car and the car hitched to it. The outlaws then gathered up cash, four packages of jewelry, and watch parts.

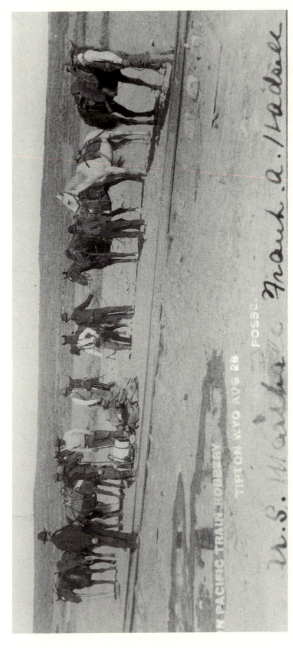

US Marshall Frank A. Hadsell and the posse, UPRR Train Robbery at Tipton, Wyoming, August 28, 1900. Wyoming State Archives, Department of State Parks and Cultural Resources, Sub Neg 10286.

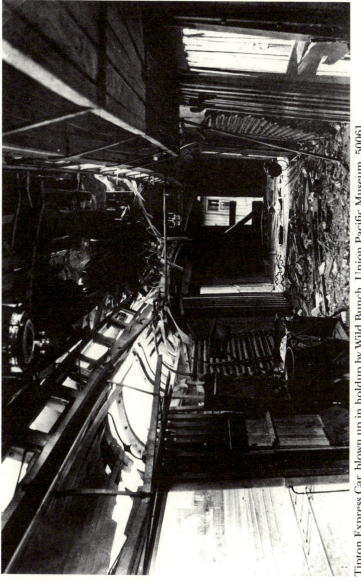

Tipton Express Car, blown up in holdup by Wild Bunch. Union Pacific Museum, 50061.

Charles E. Woodcock. Union Pacific Museum, 10166.

The Union Pacific Railroad originally claimed that only $50.40 in cash was stolen, but the railroad superintendent later admitted the amount taken was $55,000. One 14-carat gold diamond ring was valued by the railroad at $89.59.

In barely more than an hour, the thieves escaped in a southeasterly direction, and the train continued on to Green River. According to the Pinkerton files, Charles Tucker's ranch in Slater, Colorado, was used as a hideout, as was Jim

Ferguson's Battle Mountain Ranch. Both men were long-time friends of Harry Alonzo, alias Sundance.

An alarm was quickly raised, a special train car posse was sent out, and rewards of $1,000 were immediately offered for each outlaw. Three posses gathered under the leadership of Timothy T. Keliher of the Union Pacific Mounted Rangers, U.S. Marshal Frank Hadsell, Sheriff McDaniels of Carbon County, Sheriff Swanson of Sweetwater County, and U.S. Deputy Marshal Joe LeFors. Two weeks after the robbery, the posses were still following the outlaws toward Colorado, and the only hard evidence they had yet found was Joe LeFors's discovery of money wrappers along the Little Snake River near Baggs, Wyoming. The stamped wrappers suggested the thieves had stolen a total of $55,000.

Charles Woodcock, who twice faced the guns of the Wild Bunch, remained in the employ of the Union Pacific, in fact on the same route and in the same capacity of express car messenger. After thirty years of service, he finally retired to his family home in Ogden, Utah.

In spite of the list of suspects, no arrests were made for the Tipton train robbery. And although both Sundance and Butch have often been suspected of participating in the Tipton robbery, they were actually on their way to Winnemucca, Nevada, instead. It would have been difficult at best to travel the six hundred miles from Tipton to Winnemucca, and spend time in Winnemucca casing the bank, in less than three weeks.

CHAPTER 19

Three Creek, Idaho

In 1912, a Buenos Aires, Argentina, newspaper published an account of the Winnemucca bank robbery, said to have been told previously to the writer by Sundance himself. "My funds were getting low, so I drifted over to Powder Springs, one of our numerous rendezvous; where I hoped to find some of the bunch. You bet I was glad to find two of the boys there on the same errand as myself. . . . after loafing at the Springs for a month waiting . . .we started out to take in the Winnie bank. The bunch consisted of Butch Cassidy, [Will] Carver, and myself."[1]

According to the article, Sundance "caught a freight train one night and rode out on the bummers like a hobo" from Ogden, Utah. His choice of Ogden is interesting because that was where saloonkeeper Jack Egan lived; the Pinkertons considered Egan a "warm" friend of Sundance. Sundance rode the train to Winnemucca, where he checked out the bank and the town in preparation to robbing the Winnemucca National Bank. Meanwhile, Butch and Will headed to Twin Falls, Idaho, to buy horses and wait.

Once in Winnemucca, Sundance "got a job on the street, the shovel blistered my hands but I stuck to the job for three days then quit, took my check for $7.50 to the bank to get it

cashed and also to size up the interior decorations. . . . it was
the biggest little bank I had ever seen. . . . I noticed a door in
the back of the room. After getting my pay I went in again to
see if the door was used often, or if it was kept locked during
office hours. . . . About half a block down the alley west from
the bank there was a vacant lot with a high board fence
around it, just the place to leave our horses while collecting
the legal tender. There was also a high wall around the back
of the bank."

After Sundance met up with Butch and Will in Twin
Falls, they "went to Three Creek Post Office without incident,
it was necessary to have grub cached at several different
places along the trail for use on the way back from Winnemucca. Having bought a lot of horses we were broke . . . not
having the cash to buy grub we had to hold up the store at
Three Creek."

The little ranch town of Three Creek, Idaho, was home
to Tap and Jim Duncan, brothers from Texas who were also
related by marriage to the outlaw Ketchum brothers. Ironically, the combination post office and general store that the
outlaws robbed was owned by Jim Duncan and his wife, Lizzie.
According to a local history booklet, Jim had built the rock
store with rocks quarried from the nearby creeks, and it "was
a popular gathering place".[2] Speculation is that the outlaws
had heard about the Winnemucca bank through their association with the outlaw Ketchum brothers and their Three Creek
relatives. Perhaps, too, they had heard that the Winnemucca
bank advertised almost daily on the front page of *The Silver
State* newspaper that it kept $82,000 capital on hand at all
times. The bank's own advertising made robbery tempting.

Jim and Lizzie's closest neighbor was George Moore,
who also had known the Ketchum family while he was living
in Elizabethtown, New Mexico. The history booklet states, "It
is said he furnished the horses for the Winnemucca bank
robbers, who went through this country." Whether Moore

Three Creek Store, built and owned by Jim and Lizzie Duncan

willingly furnished the horses or not is uncertain; however, he was soon missing four gray horses.

Sundance's account continues, "Not having the cash to buy grub we had to hold up the store at Three Creek, the place was run by an old man and his wife. We called on them after they had gone to bed, and the old man said he wouldn't trust us for a bill of goods, so we showed him our guns, after looking at the forty fives a half minute he said, 'Yes, I'll fill your order.' We loaded two pack horses with grub and were about to leave when the old man said, 'Boys, I've got some good hats on the top shelf, perhaps you would like one apiece.' Sure we would."

Store owners Jim and Lizzie Duncan had good reason not to trust the gang for a bill of goods; Jim probably knew that these outlaws were acquainted with the Ketchums.

CHAPTER 20

Winnemuca Bank Robbery

With Moore's four gray horses in tow, Sundance, Butch Cassidy, and Will Carver rode south through Jarbidge Canyon towards Winnemucca, Nevada. They left the grays at the Silve Ranch, about thirty miles northeast of town; the horses were to be used as a relay during their escape.[1]

On September 9, 1900, the trio made camp at George D. Bliss's C S Ranch, located about fourteen miles east of Winnemucca. The C S field bordered the old Sloan Ranch and was well supplied with water and hay. The ranch superintendent at the C S was F. J. Button, whose ten-year-old son was named Vic. Seeing cowboys and buckaroos camping out after an area roundup was nothing new to Vic, but these cowboys had an especially fast and handsome white horse that he enjoyed watching and racing.

The gang spent the next few days visiting town, asking unsuspecting youngsters about a shortcut pass to Clover Valley via Soldier's Pass, and casing the bank. Young Vic recalled telling one of the cowboys that Mr. Lee at the bank was a cranky old man. One of the cowboys responded by grabbing a big knife from his saddle and replying, "I'd just as soon stick him in the ribs."[2] Another youngster, Lee Case, recalled the strangers asking questions about the town and the routes

The First National Bank of Winnemucca, circa 1900. The Humboldt Museum.

leading into and out of the area.³ The boys exchanged information for peppermint candy from the outlaws.

On the morning of September 19, 1900, Sundance, Butch, and Will rode into town and stopped at the local bar next door to the Winnemucca National Bank for a shot of whiskey. A Pinkerton informant reported that Will Carver had run into a skunk on his way to town and smelled like a polecat; this smelly description eventually found its way onto the Pinkerton wanted posters.⁴

The trio left their horses tethered to the hitching rail behind the F. C. Robbins Mercantile store in the alley that also ran behind the bank and the bar. About noon, they entered the bank through the front door on Bridge Street with their revolvers drawn.

According to a newspaper interview with bank president George Nixon, Will Carver huddled in a blanket like a hobo and guarded the door with his Winchester carbine, Sundance, brandishing two Colts 45, herded everyone up against the bank wall; and Butch Cassidy yelled "Gentlemen, throw up your hands! Be quick about it and don't make any noise!"[5] D. V. McBride, assistant cashier; Malvin Hill, bookkeeper; and Mr. Calhoun, stenographer, quickly obeyed.

Nixon further stated that one of the outlaws, identified in Sundance's account as Butch, kicked in the door to his personal office in the rear of the bank where he was discussing business with a horse buyer named W. S. Johnson. Butch brandished a large knife and threatened them with a close shave unless they opened the vault safe. Nixon quickly complied and handed Butch three bags of gold coins, worth about $5,000 each. Along with the loose cash from the office drawer and from behind the counter, the outlaws swept up a total of $32,640—$31,000 in $20 gold coins, $1,200 in $5 and $10 gold coins, with the balance in paper currency.

The outlaws then marched all five hostages out the back of the bank into the fenced yard area just off the alley; they jumped over the fence, ran up to their horses, and tied the gold-laden sacks onto their horses. In less than five minutes, they had completed their daring robbery and mounted their horses to escape. Nixon raced back into the bank, grabbed a revolver, and ran out the front door shooting into the air as an alarm. Meanwhile, Johnson also grabbed what he later described as a "pumping gun" and shot off a few rounds. Neither man hit anything except a window in the saloon next door.

According to the news coverage, the outlaws raced down the alley and turned onto Third Street; as they hit Bridge Street, they turned and crossed over the railroad tracks. With all the gunshots, a number of curious townspeople ventured out; a few gave chase on foot and yet no one was hit. One older couple who had been complaining earlier to the outlaws that the town was not lively enough was "good-naturedly" peppered with three shots aimed for their feet.[6] Hearing the gunfire, Sheriff Charles McDeid exited from the Reception

Saloon just as the thieves raced past Second Street; he took a "wing-shot" from the thieves. Still, no one was injured.

Suddenly a sack of $20 gold coins fell and spilled out onto the street. According to Sundance's version of the story, "Butch dropped the wadbag, which bursted when it dropped to the ground. The bay mare seemed to go straight up when she lost the weight. . . . while Butch and I was scraping up the yellow boys and putting them in a new sack, [Carver] smoked the posse out of sight with a 30 U.S. After making the bag fast to the saddle we hit the sand again, leaving five or six thousand dollars in the street."

Deputy Sheriff George Rose ran to the town windmill, climbed it, and took a few shots at the fleeing robbers as they headed east out of town on the Golconda Road, which ran parallel to the railroad tracks and the river. When he descended, he and a few others raced to the nearby siding, where a Southern Pacific switch engine was parked. Although the engine had to build up steam and Rose had to obtain permission to gain access to the main railroad line, the impromptu posse quickly closed the gap on the thieves and wounded Sundance's horse.

Pursuit ended, according to *The Silver State*, when the steam pipe on the engine was hit, causing a huge cloud of steam to envelop the engine. The final score? Posse, one horse. Outlaws, one train. The newspaper article reportedly dictated by Sundance ended sardonically, "Chased by a locomotive—who'd thought of that."

The outlaws made an unplanned stop at their campsite next to the Sloane Ranch, about eight miles from town, to exchange horses. With one horse wounded, they needed a replacement. They also took two horses, including a big black that belonged personally to George Nixon. The bank president later commented, "This was the unkindest cut of all . . . they robbed my bank and then stole my horse on which to escape."[7] The outlaws left two worn-out horses and raced for the shortcut to Clover Valley through Soldier's Pass, a route the youngsters of Winnemucca had described.

Meanwhile, a posse was being organized in Winnemucca, and telegrams were sent out to the nearby towns of Golconda and Tuscarora with the hope of cutting off the exit route of the thieves. However, neither town was willing at first to send out a posse without some guarantee for expenses from Winnemucca. This delayed the chase and allowed the outlaws ample time for escape.

Sundance, Butch, and Will made their first planned relay stop at the Silve Ranch, where they had previously left the four gray horses. As they carefully packed their loot and provisions onto their new mounts, they noticed the posse advancing in the distance. A ranch hand wondered out loud about the problem, and the robbers answered it was likely a posse chasing them for the Winnemucca Bank robbery. They suggested that the ranch hand tell the posse it would be unhealthy for them to continue the chase.

As they mounted their relay horses, Butch hollered to Silvian Siard, the ranch foreman, and told him to give the white horse to the kid on the C S Ranch. So Vic Button would be the new owner of an outlaw's horse.[8] Upon later examination, the youngster found that nearly all the hair had been worn off one side of the horse's neck, presumably due to the heavy sack of gold coins rubbing there.

By late afternoon, Sheriff McDeid's posse had nearly caught up to the gang. With the posse was an Indian tracker on an extremely fast pony. When he got too close, according to the local newspaper, "one of [the robbers] handed the horse he was leading to another, stopped the horse he was riding, jumped to the ground and drew his rifle from his saddle scabbard. When the Indian saw this hostile manner, he ducked behind the offside of his horse, and described a wide, fast, outward circle back toward the posse. The robber, satisfied with the effect of the demonstration, did not shoot but mounted his horse and overtook his confederates."[9]

The posse eventually gave up the chase and returned to Winnemucca. McDeid ordered "wanted" posters printed up using the descriptions supplied by George Nixon. The reward was $1,000 each for the three unknown men who were last seen headed into the Junipers, an area near Three Creek, Idaho.

Sundance asked, "How did the posse keep on our trail? There they were anyway, but with tired horses. They chased us . . . and we rode like blazes . . . Here they come again. . . . One look at the posse was enough to make us bust a hole in the atmosphere again, for them fellows back there was sure burning the breeze. . . . When we were sure that we had shaken the posse, we turned east and traveled east as fast as the tired horses could go. . . . We went around the mountain and into Idaho by an east side pass, coming out at the head of Three Creek. . . . We sat down and figured up the old man's grocery bill for groceries and hats, then doubled the amount and put it in a sack, which we left at the store as we passed that night." Outlaws though they were, they were men of their word. And they had promised Jim and Lizzie Duncan that they would pay their bill!

While Nixon worked with the Pinkertons to identify the outlaws, Sundance, Butch, and Will escaped through Three Creek. According to Sundance's news article, "We rode like blazes until noon, then stopped for lunch. Butch had just built a fire and put on the coffee pot while I had open a couple of cans of Three Creek meat. . . . We were sure that we had shaken the posse . . . coming out at the head of Three Creek. Down a little gulch where there was horse feed we divided the cleanup and as the pack horses were played out and we couldn't get to the cache in [Jarbidge], we concluded to bury the money."

Immediately following the robbery, rewards mounted upwards of $10,000, dead or alive. Once the Pinkertons were brought into the case by the American Bankers Association, they immediately recognized Sundance's alias *Alonzo* from his time in the Little Snake River Valley. And they focused their efforts upon the Wild Bunch. Locals were suspected of aiding and abetting the robbers, and mistrust fell upon a number of possible candidates, including the Frank or Dave Jones who had endorsed a check in payment for a horse.

Nixon claimed that the outlaw identified as Jones was, in fact, the outlaw who was called "Alonzo" by his partners. "We are hunting down the Dave Jones matter now. We have considerable more data that points to Jones as one of the men. For instance . . . Dave Jones sold a horse here and received a check in payment for it and gave the name of Frank Jones. I secured the signature of Dave Jones written some six months ago and the writing with Frank Jones on the back of the check is in my opinion the same . . . as I have said, it looks very much alike."[10] Nixon was again the handwriting expert in a robbery case as he had been for the Humboldt train holdup.

In the same letter, Nixon also said, "Another party [Frank Story] here who used to work with Dave Jones . . . saw him on the street the morning before the robbery. . . . when they passed two of the robbers just prior to the robbery on the street said 'there goes two of them now'. He had been telling Sam Love that the bank was to be robbed . . . that one of them was Dave Jones."

Nixon was a self-made businessman; he served as head cashier and was part owner of the Winnemucca National Bank. In later years, he became a successful rancher and served as the United States senator from Nevada. However, after the bank robbery, he played detective.

Within a few days of the robbery, a posse found the campsite at the C S Ranch that had been used by the robbers, and they thoroughly searched the area for clues. Because the outlaws had made little effort to hide their presence at the ranch, there was no trouble locating it. The posse, including Nixon, discovered three letters, torn into small pieces. Nixon carefully glued the pieces together and then sent copies of the notes to law officials and to the Pinkertons who were tracking the Wild Bunch. The three letters basically exonerated Nixon, who had been at the top of a list of possible embezzlers.

The first letter was written on August 24, 1900, and carried the law office letterhead of Douglas A. Preston, a Wyoming attorney who had befriended Butch Cassidy. The letter had no closing signature.

My dear Sir, Several influential parties are becoming interested and the chances of a sale are getting favorable.

The second letter had no heading, but the handwriting matched that of the first letter and was signed "P".

Send me at once a map of the country and describe as near as you can the place where you found that black stuff so I can go to it. Tell me how you want it handled—you don't know its value. If I can get hold of it first, I can fix a good many things favorable. Say nothing to any one about it.

The third and final letter was dated September 1, 1900, and was written to C. E. Rowe of Golconda, Nevada.

Dear Friend: Yours at hand this evening. We are glad to know you are getting along well. In regard to sale enclosed letters will explain everything. I am so glad that everything is favorable. We have left Baggs so write us at Encampment, Wyo. Hoping to hear from you soon I am as ever, Your Friend, Mike.[11]

Although the Pinkertons never definitely identified Rowe, they did discover Mike's name. On December 3, 1900, U.S. Marshal Frank P. Hadsell of Wyoming received a letter from Frank Murray of the Pinkerton's Denver office claiming that the letter signed "Mike" was actually written by a woman, further identified as Mrs. Mike Dunbar.[12] Her husband was a contact person for Sundance and Butch and was being watched by the Pinkertons; they had even given him a cipher, *Coyote*. Interestingly, her note states that the Dunbars had left Baggs and moved to Encampment. Baggs was part of the Little Snake River Valley, and Encampment was a day's ride up the mountain to the east. Sundance and Mike must have been friends when they lived and worked on the Little Snake.

At first, Nixon was not convinced that Butch Cassidy was one of the outlaws. In fact, although the robbers had been unmasked, he claimed not to recognize Butch in photographs that the Pinkertons provided. Nixon said the facial hair was hard to match; but Butch likely wore a fake beard. The Pinkertons had sent a copy of Butch's mug shot from his time in the Wyoming Penitentiary. Nixon responded, "I am trying to get a description of Cassidy from a person who formerly knew him, as the photograph you sent me is the likeness of a man with a great deal squarer cut face and massive jaws, in fact somewhat of a bulldog appearance."[13]

The person who formerly knew Butch was Tom Horn, a sometime Pinkerton agent. In a letter to Mr. J.C. Fraser of the Pinkertons, Nixon stated that he had "entered into a personal contract with" their mutual friend Horn to "run Cassidy down."[14] Horn lived and worked near the Little Snake River and likely knew Sundance as well. Nixon was also in touch with Jay L. Torrey of the M- or EmBar Ranch in Wyoming. Torrey was once a general in the Wyoming National Guard and held the rank of Colonel during the war with Spain. He reportedly knew many members of the Wild Bunch because they were interested in joining up in return for a pardon for their deeds. As such, he would be a good go-between agent. In fact, one of the abandoned horses from the holdup was a bay mare carrying the *M-* brand.[15]

However, Nixon later wrote, "So far as Cassidy is concerned we will be willing to take chances in paying the reward for him upon the evidence now in hand. . . . I am satisfied that Cassidy was interested in the robbery."[16]

Nixon's original reluctance to accept Butch Cassidy as one of the thieves caused controversy that continues in regard to Butch's participation in the holdup. However, Nixon did change his mind and was clearly satisfied that Butch was indeed involved.

Like Nixon, many Wild Bunch historians today have also changed their minds about Butch's participation, in part because of the discovery of the newspaper article from Argentina that is reportedly Sundance's account of the bank holdup. Butch also wrote a letter from South America in which he mentions that he had recently inherited some money.[17] In a clear reference to the Winnemucca bank robbery, Butch stated, "Another of my uncles died and left $30,000, Thirty Thousand, to our little family of 3, so I took my $10,000 and started to see a little more of the world."[18]

In contrast, Nixon never doubted the identity of Sundance, whom he knew as Frank Jones, alias Alonzo. Not only had Nixon heard one of the thieves use that name, but he recognized Sundance in a picture that was sent to the bank by the Pinkertons. Because no other photograph of Sundance was known at that time, this was presumably the picture that had just been taken in Fort Worth, Texas, in November 1900.

In another letter addressed to Mr. Fraser of the Pinkertons, Nixon discussed an earlier correspondence concerning both Rowe and Alonzo. "About this man Rowe, just as I told you, there is or was on Snake River a man by the name of Rowe and he was a very bad and desperate man, so the men he worked for tells me. Rowe worked for Al Reader and also for

Pinkerton's National Detective Agency.

FOUNDED BY ALLAN PINKERTON, 1850.

ROBT. A. PINKERTON, New York, } Principals.
WM. A. PINKERTON, Chicago. }

JOHN CORNISH, Manager, Eastern Division, New York.
EDWARD S. GAYLOR, Manager, Middle Division, Chicago.
JAMES McFARLAND, Manager, Western Division, Denver.

Attorneys—GUTHRIE, CRAVATH & HENDERSON, New York.

REPRESENTING THE AMERICAN BANKERS' ASSOCIATION.

OFFICES.

DENVER,
JOHN C. FRAZER, Resident Supt.

NEW YORK,
BOSTON,
MONTREAL,
BUFFALO,
PHILADELPHIA,
CLEVELAND,
CHICAGO,
ST. PAUL,
ST. LOUIS,
KANSAS CITY,
OMAHA,
PORTLAND, ORE.,
SEATTLE,
SPOKANE,
LOS ANGELES,
SAN FRANCISCO,

TELEPHONE CONNECTION.

$2,000.00 REWARD.

CIRCULAR No. 3.   DENVER, Colo., November 14th, 1904.

THE FIRST NATIONAL BANK OF WINNEMUCCA, Nevada, a member of THE AMERICAN BANKERS' ASSOCIATION, was robbed of $32,640 at the noon hour, September 19th, 1900, by three men who entered the bank and "held up" the cashier and four other persons. Two of the robbers carried revolvers and a third a Winchester rifle. They compelled the five persons to go into the inner office of the bank while the robbery was committed.

At least $31,000 was in $20 gold coin; $1,200 in $5 and $10 gold coin; the balance in currency, including one $50 bill.

Since the issuance of circular No. 1, dated Denver, Colo., May 15th, 1901, and circular No. 2, dated Denver, Colo., February 3rd, 1902, it has been positively determined that two of the men who committed this robbery were:

1. GEORGE PARKER, alias "BUTCH" CASSIDY, alias GEORGE CASSIDY, alias INGERFIELD.

2. HARRY LONGBAUGH, alias "KID" LONGBAUGH, alias HARRY ALONZO, alias "THE SUNDANCE KID."

PARKER and LONGBAUGH are members of the HARVEY LOGAN alias "KID" CURRY band of bank and train (express) "hold up" robbers.

For the arrest, detention and surrender to an authorized officer of the State of Nevada of each or any one of the men who robbed the FIRST NATIONAL BANK OF WINNEMUCCA, the following reward is offered by THE FIRST NATIONAL BANK OF WINNEMUCCA:

$1,000 FOR EACH ROBBER. ALSO 25 PER CENT, IN PROPORTIONATE SHARES, ON ALL MONEY RECOVERED.

Persons furnishing information leading to the arrest of either or all of the robbers will be entitled to share in the reward.

Below appear the photographs, descriptions and histories of GEORGE PARKER, alias "BUTCH" CASSIDY, alias GEORGIA CASSIDY, alias INGERFIELD and HARRY LONGBAUGH alias HARRY ALONZO.

Name...George Parker, alias "Butch" Cassidy, alias George Cassidy, alias Ingerfield.
Nationality...American
Occupation...Cowboy; rustler
Criminal Occupation...Bank robber and highwayman; cattle and horse thief
Age...36 yrs. (1901). Height...5 feet 9 in
Weight...165 lbs...Build...Medium
Complexion...Light. Color of Hair...Flaxen
Eyes...Blue...Mustache...Sandy if any
Remarks...Two cut scars back of head, small scar under left eye, small brown mole calf of leg. "Butch" Cassidy is known as a criminal principally in Wyoming, Utah, Idaho, Colorado and Nevada and has served time in Wyoming State penitentiary at Laramie for grand larceny, but was pardoned January 19th, 1896.

GEORGE PARKER.
From photograph taken Nov. 21, 1900.
469 P

GEORGE PARKER.
First photograph taken July 15, 1894.
432 B

Name...Harry Longbaugh, alias "Kid" Longbaugh, alias Harry Alonzo alias Frank Jones, alias Frank Boyd, alias the "Sundance Kid".
Nationality...Swedish-American.
Occupation...Cowboy; rustler
Criminal Occupation...Highwayman, bank burglar, cattle and horse thief
Age...35 years...Height...5 feet 10 in
Weight...165 to 175 lbs...Build...Good
Eyes...Blue or gray-ish...Complexion...Medium
Mustache or Beard...(if any), natural color brown, reddish tinge
Features...Grecian type...Nose...Rather long
Color of Hair...Natural color brown, may be dyed. IS BOW-LEGGED AND HIS FEET FAR APART.
Remarks—Harry Longbaugh served 18 months in jail at Sundance, Cook Co., Wyoming, when a boy, for horse stealing. In December, 1892, Harry Longbaugh, Bill Madden and Henry Bass "held up" a Great Northern train at Malta, Montana. Bass and Madden were tried for this crime, convicted and sentenced respectively; Longbaugh escaped and since has been a fugitive. June 28, 1897, under the name of Frank Jones, Longbaugh participated with Harvey Logan alias Curry, Tom Day and Walker Punteney in the Belle Fourche, South Dakota, bank robbery. All were arrested, but Longbaugh and Harvey Logan escaped from jail at Deadwood, October 31, the same year. Longbaugh has not since been arrested.

HARRY LONGBAUGH.
Photograph taken Nov. 1900.
470 P

Officers are warned to have sufficient assistance and to be fully armed, when attempting to arrest either of these outlaws, as they are always heavily armed, and will make a determined resistance before submitting to arrest, not hesitating to kill, if necessary.

This circular cancels circulars No. 1 and 2, issued by us from Denver, Colo., May 15th, 1901 and February 3rd, 1902, respectively.

IN CASE OF AN ARREST immediately notify PINKERTON'S NATIONAL DETECTIVE AGENCY at the nearest of the above listed offices.

Or   Pinkerton's National Detective Agency,

JOHN C. FRAZER,   Opera House Block, Denver, Colo.
Resident Supt., DENVER, COLO.

Pinkerton wanted poster for the Winnemucca robbery

Ora Haley . . . both these men say he is a bad man. . . . I call your attention to the reply made by [Jack] Ryan to Mr. Murray. . . . 'he [Sundance] is a fellow that used to work upon Snake River breaking horses for Reeder [*sic*] and others.'"[19] That statement suggests that Rowe and Sundance were the same person. Because Sundance arrived in Winnemucca earlier than Butch and Carver, he could easily have picked up mail at the Golconda post office. The identity of Rowe has never been discovered. He appeared just prior to the robbery and disappeared immediately following, just as Sundance had done.

In another letter from Nixon to Pinkerton agent Fraser, Nixon mentioned his recent experience in working with Tom Horn. "Horn told [Colonel E. J.] Bell that he was well acquainted with Rowe. . . . he knew him to be what was considered a bad man." Bell was said to have "a high opinion" of Horn. On Bell's recommendation, Horn went to Winnemucca to meet with Nixon. "He spent a couple of days here going over the case with me. . . . He knows several friends of Cassidy, one by the name of Jack Ryan. . . . [He claims] that Ryan has plenty of money and has gone on a trip to Arizona, and that he thinks he has gone to meet Cassidy. . . . He also knows Mike Dunbar and believes him to be, without question, the 'Mike' who wrote the letter to C. E. Rowe."[20]

In a later letter to Fraser, Nixon wrote: "About this man Rowe, just as I told you . . . he is a fellow that used to work upon Snake River breaking horses for Reader and others, and I have not seen him for about three years."[21]

CHAPTER 21

Blackened Gold

The three outlaws apparently separated in Three Creek, Idaho, although that is not fully explained in the Argentina article by Sundance. Sundance and Butch retrieved their buried gold and headed southeast to Utah and Wyoming. They exchanged the heavy, blackened gold for lighter paper currency all along the way. The Pinkertons were not very far behind them.

Pinkerton agent Frank Murray told Nixon that the bank robber known as Alonzo (Sundance) was a man also known around Rawlins as *Swede*. He stated, "About six weeks ago Swede came into Rawlins with a lot of gold coin that seemed to be blackened or burned considerably. He knew [Jack] Ryan and tried to have Ryan exchange the gold for him."[1] According to Murray, Ryan reported that over $1,400 worth of the blackened gold had been exchanged by local gamblers in his Home Ranch Saloon and by a rancher from the Dixon, Wyoming, area. In a letter to the Pinkertons, Nixon said he had heard that Ryan was "a gambler and saloon keeper at Rawlins, Wyoming. . . . Ryan has plenty of money."[2] It would appear that Ryan took his cut off the top. He took an option to buy the Club Saloon and Gambling Hall on December 12, 1900.

Although Ryan's actions were highly suspicious, the Pinker-tons were unable to prove that he had personally played any part in the exchanges that took place in his saloon. However, Ryan was well known to the Pinkertons as a contact for Sundance and the gang. After the Tipton train robbery, Pinkerton interviews indicated that Ryan "should be arrested as accessory before and after the fact." The fact that Ryan was so willing to talk with Hadsell and the Pinkertons may well have been part of the Pinkertons' decision to overlook Ryan's suspicious behavior.

In another letter to Hadsell, dated December 29, 1900, Murray revealed, "Jack Ryan told me that the man who had the money at Rawlins was Swede . . . and he might also be the third man in the Winnemucca robbery."[3] Charley Crouse, a rancher in Brown's Park and a friend to the outlaws, was also suspected of handling some of the gold; another report had the outlaws exchanging gold in a saloon in Thermopolis, Wyoming. Clearly, Sundance and Butch were laundering the heavy gold coin in every town and saloon they came to along the way.

Because some of the gold was in a "blackened" condition, it must not all have been Winnemucca gold coin; it was probably the gold coin from the Wilcox train robbery on June 2, 1899. A great deal of dynamite had been used during the Wilcox holdup, and some damage to the money would have been possible, if not likely. It should also be remembered that the Union Pacific superintendent W. L. Park later admitted that the railroad had lost more than $50,000, some of it in gold. A quick "sale" of the previously hidden blackened gold would give Sundance and Butch a better start to finance their planned trip out of the country.

After exchanging as much of the heavy, blackened gold as possible, Sundance and Butch made a brief stop at Powder Springs. As Nixon observed, "There were some men who were located some where on Powder Springs, or Powder Creek,

Wyo, who were seen to divide a large amount of gold coin. . . . they have a gang of men located whom they suspect as being our men, but intimates that it will be a very difficult matter to get them out."[4]

Sundance and Butch rode over to the Little Snake River Valley where Sundance once lived. On the night of October 25, 1900, they spent the night at Robert McIntosh's general store in Slater, Colorado; where Sundance visited with Dave Gillespie, the store clerk. Dave asked his friend, whom he knew as Alonzo, if the rumors were true that he was riding with Butch Cassidy and the Wild Bunch, robbing banks and holding up trains. Sundance admitted helping to rob the bank in Winnemucca: "He told of dropping one money bag and getting off his horse to pick up the money bag while a posse was following. He said he exchanged shots with the posse, then he went on and caught up with the others."[5] Dave's son later wrote in his memoirs: "That night, Lonzo [Sundance] went back into the store with Dad where the two of them visited for 'quite a while'. . . . [he] paid Dad back money he'd borrowed from him, laying a gold coin on the counter and saying, 'Keep the change.'"[6]

After introducing Butch to Dave and another friend, probably Jesse Galloway, they all left for the two- or three-day ride south to Walcott, Colorado, where Sundance and Butch boarded a train for Fort Worth, Texas.[7] The outlaws gave their horses and equipment, including Sundance's .30 caliber, 1895 Winchester, to their companions. They also mentioned that their final destination was going to be South America, where they planned to start a new life.

CHAPTER 22

Rendevous in Fort Worth

Sundance and Butch realized that the time had come for them to make a change—all their friends and associates were either being killed or caught and jailed. As the new century began, the breakup of their gang seemed inevitable.

Their intention truly was to go straight in a new country. In the article published in *The Standard*, Sundance states, "When the sheriffs of fourteen western states and Pinkerton Detectives read this title, they will put their ears to the ground and go off on a hot trail after yours truly . . . for I know those fellows and know they have a way of sticking to a trail once they have found it that makes a hunted man wish he hadn't done the act. . . . all were gone except a few of us; most of them went with their boots on. . . . The man hunters never let up. . . . it is a game that once you button into, the law won't let you break away from, unless you go to jail."

A. G. Francis, a friend from Bolivia, said that Sundance "told me once that he had made several attempts to settle down to a law-abiding life, but these attempts had always been frustrated by emissaries of the police and detective agencies getting on his track."[1]

Other friends claimed that Butch also felt the same way. When writer James D. Horan interviewed Percy Seibert, who had worked with Butch and Sundance in Bolivia, Seibert claimed that Butch's dream was to live a normal life. With each successful robbery, the two outlaw friends accumulated cash and gold toward their goal of retiring from their dangerous line of work, getting out of the country, and going straight. Years later, an acquaintance in Argentina wrote, "I learned that they were famous robbers of trains and banks in North America. . . . they resolved to go straight."[2]

Before they left the country, however, Sundance and Butch met up with some of their gang for a farewell party in Fort Worth, Texas. They each arrived in Fort Worth separately, Sundance and Butch via the Texas & Pacific passenger station, also called the Union Depot, on the corner of East Twelfth and Pecan streets.

In 1900, Fort Worth already had streetcars, some electric lights, and even a few of Henry Ford's first automobiles. But it was also still a railhead city, one that offered a full spectrum of entertainment and nightlife for the gang's final hurrah. Large herds of cattle, shipped through the Fort Worth stockyards, brought many cowboys and cattlemen into the city. Amid this transient population, the outlaws found anonymity, especially in Hell's Half Acre, the red-light district of the city.

By early November, Sundance and Butch had met up with Will Carver, Ben Kilpatrick, and Harvey Logan. They settled into rooms at the Maddox Hotel at 1014½ Main Street. Managed by Elizabeth "Lizzie" Maddox, the furnished apartments on the second floor of the building were available for short-term lease. Lizzie's new husband, Kendall C. Maddox, ran a small gaming room out of their personal apartment. The presence of Lizzie's teenaged son, Robert A. Archiball, probably gave a domestic aspect to an otherwise seedy area.

A few blocks away, at 705 Main Street, photographer John Swartz ran a portrait studio named Swartz View Company that featured a second-floor studio with a skylight, as well as a large display window in the ground floor office. An idea soon began to formulate among the gang members—a group picture would be a fun memento of their times and escapes together.

On Wednesday, November 21, 1900, Sundance, Butch, Will, Ben, and Harvey sat for a studio portrait, all decked out in their Sunday best. Duded up though they were, their shoes were dusty and worn, as the photograph by Swartz clearly shows. Instead of settling for one of the cheaper and more common tintype photographs, they each ordered 6½ by 8½ prints to be made using a new dry-plate processing method. They were to pick up the pictures later that week.

When the camera shutter snapped, the picture known today as the "Fort Worth Five" immediately began to make history. As author James D. Horan once wrote, the Wild Bunch "disappeared in the dust of hoofbeats, the crash of six-shooters, and . . . the efficiency of the twentieth century."[3] With their faces recorded on film, their demise began.

Apparently proud of his work, Swartz made an extra print and put it on display in his front window. According to the Pinkerton archives, Fred J. Dodge, a Wells, Fargo & Company detective, passed by and recognized Will Carver as a known outlaw. Presuming the others were also outlaws, Dodge ordered fifty prints to be made for himself. He then returned to his office, just one block up at 817 Main Street, and began the process of identifying each of the other four men. Dodge also mailed a copy to the Pinkertons, who in turn sent one to George Nixon in Winnemucca.[4]

Meanwhile, unaware of the flurry of legal activity around them, on December 1st, the gang celebrated the wedding of Will Carver and Callie May Hunt, a San Antonio prostitute known also as Lillie Davis. The couple had applied for their wedding license at the beautiful new Tarrant County Courthouse located a few blocks up Main Street.

In a later interview with the Pinkertons, Callie May acknowledged that she had seen all five of the gang earlier at the

Hole in the Wall Gang (Fort Worth Five), November 21, 1900. Left to right: Harry Longabaugh (Sundance Kid), Will Carver, Ben Kilpatrick, Harvey Logan (Kid Curry), and Robert LeRoy Parker (Butch Cassidy). Photograph by John Swartz. Denver Public Library, Western History Collection, Z-49.

Maddox apartments. She also recalled that the gang left town rather abruptly after recognizing someone, probably Dodge, on the street.

Also interviewed by the Pinkertons was Fanny Porter, the madam who employed Callie May. Fanny ran a house of prostitution at 505 South San Saba Street in San Antonio, Texas.[5] Fanny's San Antonio house was a favorite stop for the Wild Bunch, preferred over the Fort Worth house of another madam, Mary Porter. The same last name of the two madams has occasionally caused confusion over the years. Not only did Will meet Callie May at Fanny's San Antonio house but Harvey Logan and Maud Delia Moore, alias Annie Rogers, also met there.

When the Pinkertons interviewed Fanny, they gave her the cipher *Hen* in their files. She told the Pinkertons everything she could recall about her outlaw clients, including her recollections of Sundance. "Fanny Porter knows Harry Longbaugh [*sic*]. He used to have a gold tooth in front, left side, but he had it taken out and white one placed in its stead." It's interesting that Fanny mentioned Sundance's tooth; it was also mentioned in the wanted poster after Malta. "Teeth white and clean with small dark spot on upper front tooth . . ."[6]

After recognizing someone on the streets of Fort Worth, the outlaw pals hurriedly separated, with Sundance and Butch agreeing to meet in New York City in time for their departure to Argentina. But first, Sundance went to visit Ethel.

Although no wedding license has ever been found, Sundance told his family and friends that he and Ethel were indeed married; everyone in Argentina would know them as Mr. and Mrs. Place; and even the Pinkertons referred to her as Mrs. Longabaugh. Believing that she was from Texas, the Pinkertons wrote to J. H. Maddox, chief of police in Fort Worth, and asked him "to try to learn through some of your acquaintances in Texas who this woman is and where she came from."[7]

Traveling as Mr. and Mrs. Harry A. Place, they headed north for a visit with Sundance's family. They arrived in Pennsylvania at the same Phoenixville Railroad depot that young Harry had left in 1882. This was his first visit home in nearly twenty years; it was also the first time the family met Ethel.

His parents had both died. His brother Elwood still lived in California; but his sister Samanna was living in Mont Clare, sister Emma lived in Philadelphia; and brother Harvey was nearby in Flourtown. Samanna was especially pleased to know that Sundance was planning to go straight once he arrived in Argentina. They had a delightful time together, one that remained in Samanna's memory for the rest of her life. Emma continued to frown upon her brother's reputation; in fact, she changed the spelling of her last name to Longabough. After all, having an outlaw for a brother wasn't good for her seamstress business.

CHAPTER 23

Tourists in New York

Sundance and Ethel left Pennsylvania by mid-January 1901 and again headed north. He mentioned to his family that he had sustained a pistol shot wound in his left leg while out west and would be seeing a doctor. A Pinkerton report indicates that both Sundance and Ethel soon checked into Dr. Pierce's Medical Institute in Buffalo, New York.[1]

Headed by Dr. Ray V. Pierce and his brothers Dr. R. Vaughn Pierce and Dr. V. Mott Pierce, the hospital specialized in therapy and medications that today would be considered holistic healing methods. Their advertised specialty was for "treatment of all chronic diseases—particularly those of a delicate, obscure, complicated, or obstinate character." This led the Pinkertons to speculate that the couple had a venereal disease and that Ethel had been a prostitute in Texas. However, his dossier also recorded that Sundance had severe catarrh, a sinus condition; and he had mentioned his gunshot wound to his family. Their actual treatment was not recorded for the Pinkertons, and the hospital records do not exist today.

However, the hospital did send a brief report to the Pinkertons: It remains our best description of both Sundance and Ethel. Dated May 1902, it reads,

Dr. Pierce's Invalids Hotel. Buffalo and Erie County Historical Society.

Harry Longbaugh [sic] alias Harry A. Place. About 35, 5 ft 9, 185 or 190. Med Comp. Brown eyes, Lt Bro hair. Lt Bro or Sandy Mustache, feet Small. not bow legged—both feet turns in walking. face much tanned with the Sun. Mrs. Harry A. Place age 23 or 24—5 ft 5. 110#. Med Comp medium dark hair Blue or gray eyes regular features. No marks or blemishes.[2]

On February 1, 1901, Mr. and Mrs. Harry Place arrived with Butch Cassidy, alias James Ryan, and signed the guest register at Mrs. Catherine Taylor's boarding house, located at 234 West Twelfth Street. They rented a second-floor suite overlooking the street for three weeks, paying cash up front. According to census records, Mrs. Taylor's house was quite large; the house contained twenty rooms, and she employed a chef and two servants.[3] Mrs. Taylor's husband George had recently died, and her thirteen-year-old son John helped her run the rooming house, which could hold up to twenty-five boarders. Sundance posed as a cattle buyer from Wyoming, accompanied by his wife, along with his wife's "brother."

They visited all the sights in the city, and that brought about an angry memo from William Pinkerton to his brother Robert that complained about the agency's "looking for them in the mountains and wilderness" while the outlaws were instead acting like "tourists in New York."[4]

On February 3, 1901, Sundance and Ethel posed for a portrait at the DeYoung Photography Studio, located at 826 Broadway, possibly as a wedding memento. Sundance immediately mailed a copy of the photo back to David Gillespie in the Little Snake River Valley along with a letter "from New York City, with a picture of him and his wife, saying he had married a Texas lady he had known previously."[5] Presumably, he also mailed a copy home to his family; however, the picture never arrived in Pennsylvania. Within sight of Samanna's home in Mont Clare, the post office kept the Pinkertons informed of all communications. It is believed by the family that a postal clerk confiscated the photo and turned it over to the Pinkertons. A notation in Sundance's file states, "We have ordered copies of a photograph which Longbaugh [sic] had taken of himself and the woman . . . said to be his wife and to be from Texas." That picture soon appeared on many wanted posters.[6]

The trio also made a visit to Tiffany's Jewelers on the corner of Fifteenth Street and Union Square. On February 4, 1901, Butch purchased a beautiful gold watch for $40.10, serial number 68210-1685. Was it a wedding gift? Later, an acquaintance in South America claimed that Sundance had "a very fine Tiffany gold watch that his partner Butch Cassidy had purchased on his way thru New York City enroute to South America."[7] The date of purchase suggests that it could not have been the lapel watch worn by Ethel in her photograph

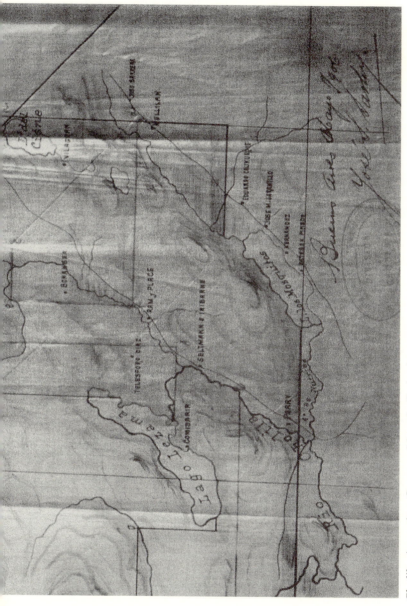

Cholila, Argentina. Courtesy Marcelo Gavirati.

on February 3rd. The threesome spent their evenings riding in horse-drawn carriages around the park in Union Square and past the outskirts of what is now Greenwich Village.

There is also a record in the Pinkerton files that Sundance took treatment with a Dr. Weinstein in New York City.[8] The 1900 and 1902–1903 New York City directories list Dr. Isaac Weinstein's office at 174 Second Avenue. Dr. Weinstein's name is also found in the 1896 and 1897 directories of the Public Medical Society of the County of New York. He is listed as a physician at St. Marks Hospital, the New York Eye and Ear Hospital that was located across the street at 177 Second Avenue. It would be reasonable to suggest that Sundance was seeking treatment for his catarrh. Interestingly, one of Dr. Weinstein's partners trained at the University of Buffalo; that suggests Sundance may have learned of Dr. Weinstein during his stay at Dr. Pierce's Invalids Hotel in Buffalo.

On February 20, 1901, Sundance and Ethel boarded the R. P. Houston Company ship *Herminius;* the British ship left New York the following morning and headed for Buenos Aires, Argentina. They traveled as Mr. and Mrs. Harry Place. Although some researchers believe that Butch returned west for one final robbery, evidence in Argentina suggests that Butch traveled with them, under the name James Ryan.[9]

CHAPTER 24

Going Straight in Argentina

The *Herminius* arrived in Buenos Aires, Argentina, on March 23, 1901.[1] Mr. and Mrs. Harry Place disembarked and temporarily settled into the Hotel Europa, a fashionable and popular hotel in the center of the thriving city. Sundance visited the London and River Plate Bank where he deposited two thousand pounds in gold notes, worth about $12,000 at the time. He gave his residence as the Hotel Europa and used the alias Harry Place.

By all indications, Sundance intended to settle down on a ranch and live a peaceful life with his wife, Ethel; he was going to be a law-abiding rancher. Sundance and Butch asked the advice of the U.S. vice-consul, Dr. George Newbery, a Buenos Aires dentist who was an American immigrant from New York. Newbery suggested Cholila, a sparsely settled area with good grass that he hoped would become a colony of transplanted Americans. Sundance and Butch also learned that Cholila was near the border of Chile, nestled into the foothills of the Andes Mountains, on the east bank of the Blanco River, over four hundred miles from the nearest railroad, and without a telegraph—all positives to outlaws seeking peace and quiet.[2]

Hotel Europa as seen from a ship in Buenos Aires

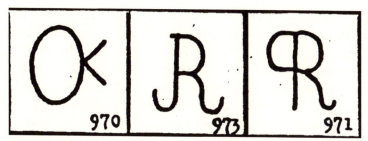

Detail from Chubut brand registration book. Courtesy Dan Buck and Anne Meadows.

The trio liked what they saw in Cholila, and began building up their small ranch. On June 11, 1901, Sundance and Butch purchased "16 colts from an estancia near Cholila with a $855 check drawn on the Banco de Londres y Rio de la Plata. In October, 1901, they registered their brands in Rawson, the Chubut capital."[3] Sundance registered *O<* under his alias Enrique A. Place; Butch registered an *R* under his alias Santiago Ryan; and together Butch and Sundance registered a reversed *P* superimposed with an *R* for Place and Ryan.

On March 1, 1902, nearly a year after arriving in Argentina, Sundance and Butch applied to homestead four leagues of land in Cholila. A month later, on April 2, 1902, Butch finalized the application for "four square leagues of Government land within the Province of Chubut, district 16th of II October, near Cholilo [*sic*]."[4]

While Butch was filling out all the paperwork in Buenos Aires, Sundance and Ethel boarded the S.S. *Soldier Prince* on March 3, 1902, and returned for a visit to the States. They arrived back in New York City on April 3, 1902, and registered at Mrs. Thompson's rooming house, located at 325 East Fourteenth Street. During this visit, according to the Pinkertons, they spent part of their time at Coney Island, a popular beach and amusement park of the day, just outside New York City.

They also took the hundred-mile train ride to visit the family in Pennsylvania. Samanna's family remembered that Sundance invited her two sons to visit them in Cholila. The recently opened Willow Grove Park was only about twenty miles from Samanna's home in Mont Clare; it seems likely they would have visited the amusement park to hear John Phillip Sousa's band play. Sundance and Ethel also spent time with the family of his brother Harvey, who was working at the beach resort town of Atlantic City, New Jersey, at the time. By June, however, they returned to New York City and made another purchase at Tiffany's Jewelers. On June 25, Sundance paid $15.35 for a watch, serial no. 2590-1128643.[5]

Once again, the family was told of an old gunshot injury for which Sundance may have sought treatment in the Chicago area. It also may have been a return visit to the clinic in Buffalo, which would have coincided with the May 10, 1902, date on the report sent to the Pinkertons.

However, the Pinkerton files place Sundance in the Chicago area during the summer of 1902.[6] On July 3, 1902, the Chicago–Rock Island Railroad Express no. 5 was held up by two men near Dupont, Illinois. The take was only about $500, some jewelry, and a few other items of lesser value. The safe was not blown, although a bag of dynamite was later found nearby.

A hobo who was free-riding on the train reportedly recognized a photograph of Sundance as one of the thieves, which brought the Pinkertons into the chase. However, it seems doubtful that Sundance could have participated in the robbery and still be in New York City in time for his return to Argentina just one week later.

On July 10, 1902, Mr. and Mrs. Harry Place sailed out of New York harbor on board the steamer *Honorius*. This ship, however, was actually a freighter, and did not normally carry passengers; therefore, Sundance hired on as purser, and Ethel

Hotel Touring Club. The left side of this building was the Del Globo Hotel.

was listed as steward. They arrived back in Buenos Aires on August 9, 1902, and again checked into the Hotel Europa.

Sundance closed out his bank account there on August 14, 1902, and a day later he and Ethel boarded the S.S. *Chubut*, a small steamer. They traveled first by boat along the Atlantic coast and then the remainder of the way by pack mule and horseback. It was not an easy trip, but they were headed home. An unsigned and undated memo in the Pinkerton files describes the trip.

> To reach it [the ranch] from Buenos Aires, would be by steamboat to Bahia Blanca, thence by smaller boat from Bahia Blanca to Rawson on the coast at the mouth of the Chubute [*sic*] River. From there on horseback to the 16th d'October district. Distance from rawson to 16 d'October 200 miles, probably two weeks travel. Fare New York to Buenos Aires to Bahia Blanca and thence to Rawson $160 in gold. Steamers run twice

a month. Horse at Rawson cost $50, wagon $200, provisions for two weeks $100.

During their travels, Sundance and Ethel frequently stayed in the hotel Del Globo, in the Welsh settlement of Trelew near Rawson; the hotel was managed by their good friend Angel M. Botaro.[7] In the Pinkerton files is a report that Botaro cashed a check for Butch worth $3,546, drawn on the London & River Platte Bank account on May 16, 1902.

CHAPTER 25

Mistaken Identity

While Sundance, Ethel, and Butch were settling into their new home in Argentina, Sundance was being accused of the July 3, 1901, train robbery in Wagner, Montana. In fact, the authorities in St. Louis, Missouri, thought they were holding him in their local jail.

On November 5, 1901, the St. Louis police arrested Ben Kilpatrick for passing stolen bank notes. He refused to identify himself or to answer any questions. When searching his pockets, the authorities found a key to the Laclede Hotel, where Ben and his girlfriend Laura Bullion were staying. The following morning, the police arrested Laura, who was about to leave with a satchel full of forged bank notes.

Both Ben and Laura remained silent; they were not anxious to reveal their true names. So the St. Louis police contacted the Pinkerton Detective Agency and received "wanted" circulars from Wagner. They soon believed they were holding Harry Longabaugh, alias the Sundance Kid, based upon the description from the Pinkertons.

The police went through Laura's belongings. The *Daily Globe Democrat* reported: "In a notebook found among Miss Bullion's personal effects were written these lines: Harry Longbaugh [*sic*] very black hairs, steel gray eyes, very fair skin when not tanned by the sun."[1] They questioned Laura about her companion, and she answered, "I have known the prisoner whom you call Longbaugh [*sic*] since the latter part of last April."[2]

Laura also reportedly claimed that she "found in his coat a pocket dictionary, on the fly of which was written the name 'Harry Longuebaugh' [*sic*]." She asked him "if this was another of his names and he replied evasively."[3] The police were definitely convinced that they had captured the Sundance Kid.

It was not until November 15, 1901, that Ben Kilpatrick was correctly identified; Sundance was no longer in custody in St. Louis, Missouri. And they never knew that he was already ranching peaceably in Argentina with his wife, Ethel Place, and with Butch Cassidy.

CHAPTER 26

Cholila, Home Sweet Home

Sundance and Ethel clearly made a new home for themselves in Argentina. Their ranch consisted of a spacious four-room cabin as the main house, a stable, chicken coop, a smaller bunkhouse for the native cowhands, and what Butch referred to as a "wearhouse."[1] As the ranch business grew, they even built a small store for their neighbors and ranch hands. Although Sundance, Ethel, and Butch likely lived together in the four-room cabin originally, there is some local evidence that Butch also built a bachelor's pad for himself.[2]

Primo Caprara, an Italian who once spent the night in Cholila and then wrote about it, seemed impressed. He spoke of them as peaceful ranchers.

> The house was simply furnished and exhibited a certain painstaking tidiness, a geometric arrangement of things, pictures with cane frames, wallpaper made of clippings from North American magazines . . . many beautiful weapons and lassos braded from horse hair. . . . The lady, who was reading, was well-dressed. I had a friendly dinner. . . . she kept perfumed water in the house's wash basins, spoke some Spanish.

Later, I learned that they were famous robbers of trains and banks in North America.[3]

Their neighbors seemed to accept them, even those who knew of their past as outlaws. "Their law-abiding activities, their proper manners and their pleasant disposition soon led them to be held in high regard by neighbors and authorities," wrote Marcelo Gavirati.[4] After a local party on March 9, 1904, for the territorial governor Dr. Julio Lezana, one neighbor observed, "They were not good mixers, but whatever they did was correct . . . no one suspected they were criminals."[5] According to Gavirati, "The governor was entertained by three of the most respectable neighbors, Americans James Ryan and Mr. and Mrs. Harry Place. . . . Hospitality the governor accepted, staying overnight at the cabin of the trio of American ranchers in Cholila."[6]

Clearly, Sundance, Ethel, and Butch had made a home together in Cholila. Shortly before Sundance and Ethel returned to Cholila from their visit in the States, Butch wrote a letter dated August 10, 1902, to his friend Matilda Davis in Utah.

I visited the best Cities and best parts of the countrys of South A. till I got here, and this part of the country looked so good that I located, and I think for good. for I like the place better every day. I have 300 cattle, 1500 sheep, and 28 good Saddle horses, 2 men to do my work, also good 4 room house, wearhouse [sic] stable, chicken house and some chickens.[7]

Because he was now in a law-abiding life style and in a settled home, Sundance and his sister Samanna began writing to each other more frequently.[8] She kept her husband's business records, and she occasionally entered a personal note under the daily headings of the accounting book in a diary format. On July 22, 1902, she wrote to her brother; she wrote again on January 3, 1903; and he answered. What Samanna never knew was that their letters were often read by local postal clerks who had been hired as informants by the Pinkertons; the law now had a clue as to the whereabouts of Sundance and Butch.

In early March of 1903, Pinkerton agent Frank P. Dimaio finished an assignment in Brazil and was sent to Argentina to see if he could locate the outlaws. Upon arriving in Buenos Aires, he interviewed Dr. George Newbery, who had met the outlaw trio when they originally landed in Argentina. Newbery said that from the photographs he recognized Butch and Sundance as his neighbors 130 miles south of his ranch. However, he told Dimaio "that it would be impossible to apprehend these criminals at that time due to the fact that about May 1st the rainy season would set in and the country would become so flooded it would be impossible for the authorities to reach Cholila and bring about their arrest. That in order to reach Cholila it would be necessary to go to Puerto Madryn, 250 miles south of Buenos Aires, and then travel by horseback for about 15 days through the jungle. That it would be necessary to hire a peon familiar with the trail. Upon arrival in Cholila the commandant of the garrison at the 16th October would have to be seen and the arrangements made for the arrest of these criminals."[9]

So, instead of traveling to Cholila, Dimaio contacted the local Buenos Aires authorities and warned them of the presence of American outlaws in their midst. He then flooded the area with wanted posters written in Spanish, and set up a code to be used in communicating with the Pinkertons.

Under the heading of *Castleman, New York,* Newbery and local authorities were to wire the Pinkertons of a shipment of fruit: *Longabaugh = lemons, Cassidy = citron, L & wife = apricots. Mrs. L = peaches, L wife & Cassidy = oranges, sailed on = Pears.* These new cipher names replaced earlier names used in the States; Sundance had been *Sand* and Butch had been *Primer.*[10]

The *Tea Party*. © Paul D. Ernst.

Not knowing that they had been discovered, Ethel and Sundance once again returned to the States. They must not have liked cold weather—with the seasons reversed in the Southern Hemisphere, they often traveled north around March to enjoy a warmer climate in the States. Or maybe Ethel was just homesick for her family. In any event, a Pinkerton memo mentions that they were believed to have been in the area of Baggs, Wyoming, sometime in 1903.[11]

A year later, on February 29, 1904, Butch wrote a short letter that mentioned Sundance's intention to go to the Lake on March 1st to buy bulls. This was probably Lake Nahuel Huapi in Rio Negro, a few days' ride north where their friend Jared Jones, an American from Texas, had a large estancia or ranch. This trip was about the same time that territory governor Dr. Julio Lezana visited Sundance and Butch's home; and many of their neighbors also visited the Cholila ranch

Cholila Post Card Scenes. © Paul D. Ernst.

during the party. A number of sources mention that the new governor danced with the hostess, Mrs. Ethel Place.[12]

Because Carlos Foresti, a professional photographer, was a member of the governor's party, this may also have been the occasion for the pictures that were taken at the ranch and mailed back home to Samanna. The *Tea Party* shows Sundance and Butch seated on chairs behind their ranch house with Ethel holding a tea kettle and standing between them. The scene is quite domestic, even down to Ethel's smock apron and the two dogs sitting at their feet. The cocker spaniel was reportedly Ethel's favorite and went nearly everywhere with her.

A second photograph shows nine people standing in the front yard of the ranch, along with various horses and dogs. Clearly representing sections of one photograph, the pictures received by the family are in the format of three postcard-sized, connecting photos. The left side shows Butch and three horses; the middle section, presumably six neighbors and friends; and the right one, Sundance and Ethel standing next to their horses. Today the family refers to these as the *Cholila Post Card Scenes.* There is a second copy of the scenes in a single photograph format; it is owned today by a descendant of Jarred Jones, one of Sundance's Patagonian neighbors.[13] Somehow these photographs were all missed by the postal clerk–Pinkerton informant back home in Mont Clare and remain in the family today.

As the cold weather arrived in the Southern Hemisphere, Ethel and Sundance again headed north for the warmer temperatures in the States. It was at this time that an unsigned, wooden postcard was mailed to Emma, Sundance's sister, from the 1904 St. Louis World's Fair and Exposition.[14] It would seem that they were again acting as tourists, just taking in the sights along with millions of other anonymous visitors.

A Pinkerton memo written October 24, 1904, also placed them in the area of Fort Worth, Texas. "Our report here shows that Longbaugh [*sic*] and his wife Ethel Place are probably now in the United States. This information is partially confirmed through an informant who has been to our Denver office and reported conferences he has had with Longbaugh and his wife and Cassidy in the vicinity of Fort Worth. . . . we definitely recommend that your Protective Committee authorize us, first, to make an investigation at Fort Worth, Texas, San Antonio, Texas, and such other points."[15] But, by the time the memo was actually written, Ethel and Sundance were already home in Cholila.

On November 26, 1904, Samanna again wrote to her brother. A month later, on December 30th, Butch ordered supplies for the ranch from local merchant Richard Clarke.[16] His order totaled 18.40 pesos and included six pairs of socks, two pairs of slippers, one sweater, and two handkerchiefs. But their lives were about to change dramatically.

Cholila cabin today

About 3 P.M. on Tuesday, February 14, 1905, two English-speaking men robbed the Rio Gallegos bank.[17] The bank manager, Mr. Bishop, and the cashier, Mr. MacKareow, were forced to hand over 280 gold or sterling pesos and 23,000 in paper currency pesos. The outlaws made a clean escape and headed towards the Patagonian Andes to the north.

Police later identified the "tall, slight man and the other a shorter man, fair complexion, and both clean shave" as being "Henry Linden and Co."[18] Although immediately suspected of the holdup, Sundance and Butch did not participate. It is believed today that Robert Evans, an acquaintance of Sundance and Butch, was one of the thieves.

In mid-February of 1905, Sundance and Butch were enumerated on a Cholila Agricultural Census Survey.[19] Clearly, they were still living peaceful, law-abiding lives. One of the most important aspects of this census is that it provides an unquestionable alibi to Sundance and Butch for the bank robbery at Banco de Londres y Tarapacá in Rio Gallegos on February 14, 1905. Although they may have known about and even aided in the planning for the robbery, they definitely were not involved in the actual holdup.

The bank robbery, however, was done in typical Wild Bunch fashion, and that brought their presence in Cholila to the attention of the law. The events were now set into motion that would spell the end of their idyllic life in Cholila.

CHAPTER 27

On the Run Again

The Americans were to be brought in for questioning in connection with the Rio Gallegos bank robbery. A warrant was issued by the police chief in Buenos Aires stating, in part, "As their specialty is armed robbery of banks, trains and public buildings in broad daylight, and they were in the country . . . it is presumed they are the perpetrators."[1]

The authorities in Buenos Aires ordered Eduardo Humphries, the sheriff of Esquel, the nearest major town, to serve the arrest warrant on Sundance and Butch.[2] However, Humphries was a good friend of Sundance and Butch; and he also adored Ethel. He was later fired for insubordination because he refused to carry out the arrest order. Whether it was a message from Humphries or word sent through their ranch foreman, Daniel Gibbon, Sundance and Butch received a warning of their impending arrest. Just as in the movie scene, Butch and Sundance probably looked at each other and sighed, "So now that we've gone straight, what do we do?"

The long arm of the law had finally reached them at their little ranch in Cholila. Things began to happen quickly. On April 19, 1905, Butch wrote a note to Richard Clarke asking that his previously ordered merchandise be delivered, instead, to Dan Gibbon because he was packing to leave Cholila.[3]

Unaware of the unraveling situation in Argentina, Samanna wrote her last letter to her brother on April 22, 1905. It probably never reached him.

On May 1, 1905, Butch wrote to his nearest neighbor, John C. Perry, to say that they were all leaving Cholila *that day*. Before moving to Argentina around 1901, Perry had been the first sheriff in Crockett County, Texas. He knew the outlaw past of both Sundance and Butch, but he accepted them as friends and good neighbors in Cholila. Perry's wife, Bertie, casually wrote in a letter to a friend in Texas that they had recently visited some Texans living nearby only to discover that they were outlaws whom her husband had known in the States.[4]

In his interviews with author James D. Horan, Seibert mentioned a growing affection between Sundance and a neighbor's wife. Horan's notes read: "ranch, neighbor—deputy sheriff in west, wife, thought Sundance paying too much attention . . . neighbor had been Deputy Sheriff. knew of Butch, & didn't like wife falling for Sundance"[5] There is nothing to substantiate this rumor.

Sundance, Ethel, and Butch packed up a few of their belongings and traveled to Lake Nahuel Huapi on May 9th, accompanied by their employee and friend Wenceslao Solis. The trio sailed across the lake on the steamer *Condor* to Chile, and Solis returned to Cholila with their saddles. He began to carry out their orders to dispose of the ranch holdings.[6]

The ranch buildings and supplies were sold to Thomas T. Austin, the manager of Cochamo Company, a Chilean land and cattle company, for 18,000 pesos. The bulk of their personal belongings, including a trunk full of private letters, were left with Dan Gibbon, John Perry, Wenceslao Solis, and other good friends. Their livestock was also to be sold and the money held for them by Gibbon, their ranch foreman and friend. Because the ranch was still considered to be homesteaded property, and therefore not deeded to them, the land itself could not be sold.

On June 28, 1905, Sundance wrote to Gibbon from Valparaiso, Chile, saying that he and Ethel had arrived safely and intended to leave for San Francisco on the 30th.

Dear Friend:

We are writing to you to let you know that our business went well and we received our money. We arrived here today, and the day after tomorrow my wife and I leave for San Francisco. I'm very sorry, Dan, that we could not bring the brand R with us, but I hope that you will be able to fetch enough to pay you for the inconveniences.

We want you to take care of Davy and his wife and see that they don't suffer in any way. And be kind to the old Spaniel and give him pieces of meat once in a while and get rid of the black mutt.

I don't want to see Cholila ever again, but I will think of you and of all our friends often, and we want to assure you of our good wishes.

Attached you will find the song "Sam Bass," which I promised to write down for you. As I have no more news, I will end by begging that you remember us to all our friends, without forgetting Juan and Vencylow [sic], giving them our regards and good wishes, keeping a large portion for yourself and family.

Remaining as always your true friend,

H. A. Place[7]

Assuming that they did leave "the day after tomorrow," Ethel and Sundance left Valparaiso on June 30, 1905. Even though Valparaiso was a large seaport with an easy and direct route to San Francisco, one local police report has them traveling overland to Buenos Aires instead. A police deposition was taken in 1911 to ascertain the activities of two outlaws named Wilson and Evans. Because they were known to have associated with Butch and Sundance, the Cholila ranch trio was occasionally mentioned in the deposition. Territory of Chubut police chief Leandor Navarro summarized their activities: "The fugitives went to Chile where they boarded a steamship and sailed to Valparaiso. . . . Place and his wife [traveled] as Matthews. . . . In Valparaiso, they boarded the trans-Andean train" and traveled east towards Buenos Aires.[8]

The last time Ethel's presence can be positively verified anywhere was in the writing of Sundance's letter on June 29, 1905.[9] However, an interesting possibility has recently been discovered in New York shipping manifests.[10]

On July 29, 1905, the S.S. *Seguranca* arrived in New York City carrying 105 passengers from Colon, Panama, which was a common transfer point for those who wanted to travel through New York rather than San Francisco. (Although the Panama Canal was not yet finished, a railroad took passengers across the forty-mile isthmus between the Pacific and Atlantic oceans. This train ride might explain Navarro's statement that they traveled by train.)

On board the ship was Mrs. E. Place, an American citizen who was born in 1879. She was apparently married since she gave her name as Mrs. Place; she marked married under the single-or-married column; and she claimed to be a wife under the "occupation" column. Although she gave only an initial for her first name, the rest of the information matches Sundance's wife, Mrs. Ethel Place.

Of further interest is the unknown male listed directly above her name. Mr. R. Scott was an American citizen; he was born in 1867; he was married; and his occupation was that of a merchant. Although R. Scott would be a previously unknown alias, he easily matches what we know about Sundance.

Possibly they just changed their plans at the last minute in order to enjoy once again the sights and sounds of New

York City. Or, because their trip was unplanned, they may have discovered upon arrival in Colon that they would have to wait for a ship leaving for San Francisco, while they could board the *Seguranca* immediately. And the *Seguranca*'s departure from Colon on July 22, 1905, fits exactly right if they left Valparaiso on June 30, 1905, as the letter stated.[11]

Because Ethel is suspected of being with Sundance at the time of the Villa Mercedes bank robbery the following December, she must have returned to South America; but her friends from the Cholila ranch never saw her again. Sundance and Ethel reportedly settled into the port city of Antofagasta, Chile, where he had some "difficulty" with the Chilean authorities.

On January 26, 1906, a Pinkerton memo issued from the Philadelphia office mentioned that Sundance was using the name Frank Boyd or H. A. Brown, and he had been in trouble with the Chilean government "a short time ago." The Pinkertons' source for this information was a letter Sundance wrote to Samanna that was found by the informant in the Mont Clare, Pennsylvania, post office. No reason was given for the problem, and nothing has been found after an exhaustive search of Chilean records by present-day researchers. However, the United States vice-consul, Frank Aller, assisted Mr. Boyd/Brown in clearing up the problem at a cost of $1,500.

Mr. Aller worked for the American Smelting and Refining Company, located in Antofagasta, Chile. He also worked as vice-consul, a political go-between or trouble-shooter for Americans in foreign countries. He may not have known Sundance's true identity when he helped him out of this trouble with the Chilean authorities.

Author Horan interviewed Percy Seibert of the Concordia Mines in New York City during the 1950s about his friendship with Sundance and Butch. Although Horan's notes are abbreviated and at times difficult to read, they may contain a possible explanation for the trouble Sundance had in Chile.

List of passengers on the *Seguranca*, July 1905. Ethel Place is listed here as a passenger. U.S. National Archives, Microfilm no. T715_604.

Sundance, going back, 1905, woman, . . . restaurant posters, depicting 75000, 10,000 joked with constable if found, split . . . got stouter . . . woman started to go out. number of deputies, to pick him up—as was custom, no single action .45—use black jack or billy, cock it faster ordinary man . . . Smith Wesson lawman . . . covered man, chief police shot, no intention, accident, showed cops gun, held week, had lawyer . . . sent message to Butch, who had 1,000 English. gave bill, northern Argentina—1906 . . . picked up Sundance to help him.[12]

Obviously, no one knows what Seibert actually said, and we can only guess what Horan's notes mean. However, it is possible that Sundance and Ethel were eating dinner in a restaurant prior to leaving the country when a constable noticed a "wanted" poster of Sundance. They joked about a physical similarity and again turned to leave; more deputies entered. Sundance was concerned enough to draw his gun, even though they only had billy clubs. In the ensuing confusion, Sundance's gun accidentally fired, wounding the chief of police. He was held in the jail for a week while Aller collected $1,500 ($1,000 from Butch) to be posted as bail. This could explain the "difficulty" in Chile in which Sundance was involved.

Furthermore, if that is the explanation, then possibly Ethel returned home to the States alone, via New York City on the S.S. *Seguranca*.

CHAPTER 28

A Return to Crime

On Tuesday afternoon, December 19, 1905, the Banco de la Nación in Villa Mercedes de San Luis, Argentina, was robbed; the armed Banditos Yanqui escaped with 12,000 pesos. Witnesses immediately stated that the bandits were three men and a woman; and the bank officers identified Butch, Sundance, and Ethel from their photos on Pinkerton "wanted" posters.[1]

On December 24th, two Buenos Aires newspapers, *La Prensa* and *La Nación*, each credited the robbery to Sundance, Ethel Place, Butch, and Kid Curry. (Kid Curry was an alias that Harvey Logan used, and he was erroneously suspected of joining Butch and Sundance in South America. However, he had already died in a shootout with Colorado police on June 9, 1904.) Researchers Dan Buck and Anne Meadows believe the fourth outlaw was Robert Evans, an acquaintance of Sundance and Butch from Cholila.[2]

One newspaper described the smallest outlaw as "beardless, had small feet and delicate features . . . it is supposed that the woman was in charge of cooking the meals . . . the woman is a fine rider." Another description stated, "Miss H. A. Place . . . an interesting woman, very masculine, who wears male clothing with total correctness, and who is dedicated more to the occupation of men than to those of women . . . a fine rider, handles with precision all classes of firearms, and has an admirable male temperament."[3]

While two of the thieves covered the bank employees and a few customers, the other two rifled the bank safe. When the bank manager resisted, he was struck with the butt of a revolver, leaving him with a minor head wound. Within four minutes, the gang was once again mounted and racing out of town. A posse was quickly gathered and gave chase, and reportedly wounded one of the outlaws. When the posse drew too close for comfort, however, the bandits dismounted and fired back. A bullet striking the lead horse discouraged the posse from following so closely. The gang remounted and escaped. If this robbery included Ethel, she once again disappeared from record. That raises the possibility that she was the wounded outlaw and died from her wounds; or even suggests that she did indeed return alone to the States.

Butch and Sundance apparently went their own separate ways about this time. Butch soon took a job with the Concordia Mines in Bolivia, and Sundance found work breaking mules for Roy Letson, a contractor who was driving mules from northern Argentina to a railroad construction camp near La Paz, Bolivia. Letson found Sundance to be shy but rather likeable.

> Longabaugh kept very much to himself most of the time. I told him my destination was Bolivia and he said that he would be glad to go along. We were several weeks on that trip. . . . He was employed by our company to break the mules to harness and saddle and done a very good job . . . well dressed . . . did have a very fine Tiffany gold watch. . . . it was not long before he was on the go again.[4]

By the end of 1906, Sundance and Butch were together again, working for the Concordia Mines in the La Paz

Department, southeast of the city of La Paz, Bolivia. The mine was located 16,000 feet up in the Santa Vela Cruz Mountains, a range within the central Bolivian Andes. They were hired as payroll guards by Clement Rolla Glass, the mine manager.

Glass's assistant, Percy Seibert, met the duo at a Christmas party at the Grand Hotel Guibert in La Paz. At first, Siebert did not know of their outlaw past, but he later heard rumors. "Look here I hear you you are Yankee American bandit rumor Butch—come in and talk—light electric light—treated decent we're hole in wall gang."[5]

When he worked with them, Seibert knew Sundance as Harry Brown, and Butch as Santiago Maxwell. The three became friends, and the outlaws frequently ate Sunday dinner with Seibert's family. He described Sundance's fast and accurate shooting. "Sundance, 2 bottle of beer right—and left, hands, threw in air, draw single action revolver."[6]

Seibert recalled that Butch usually sat facing the door so that he could see anyone who might enter the house. Seibert even sketched his living quarters to show a man with his back to the rear wall. Their friendship was cemented when Butch ordered two local outlaws out of the mining camp. "Nation came in Clifford—wanted pay roll robbery—wanted gringo camp. give bad name, wanted horseshoes made, out of money, gave $50—get out!"[7] The local outlaws, Nation and Clifford, were planning a robbery because they were out of money. Butch did not want Seibert's payroll stolen, so he gave the men $50 and chased them away.

Whether from boredom or empty pockets, Sundance and Butch would occasionally leave the mines to head out on a trip. When they returned, according to Seibert, they were always flush with cash; and he would have heard rumors of another small robbery. But their work and loyalty to the Concordia was apparently above question. As in the past, they were always law-abiding and supportive to their employers.

According to Seibert, a "panic" occurred at the Concordia in 1907, and he traveled to New York for a visit for the summer. When he returned, he claimed to have paid a dime to see a moving picture of Butch from Rawlins, Wyoming, while he was on Morey's Pier at Coney Island; and when he mentioned it to Butch, they had a good laugh. "[s]ummer 1907—Perce [Seibert] in Coney Island. Morey Pier, 10 cents, picture. Rawlins, Butch Cassidy, he laughed."[8]

Sundance began drinking heavily and bragging about their outlaw past according to Seibert; and this eventually necessitated the duo leaving the Concordia. This may have been when Sundance reportedly related the story of the Winnemucca bank robbery that ended up in the newspapers after his death.

Butch sent a letter from Santa Cruz, Bolivia, to his friends at the Concordia on November 12, 1907. His letter suggested that he and Sundance were thinking of settling down again; they were going to make a final attempt at going straight. For this, they needed cash.

> To The Boys At Concordia:
>   We arrived here about 3 weeks ago after a very pleasant journey and found just the place I have been looking for 20 years and [Sundance] likes it better than I do. He says he wont try to live any where else. . . The grass is good . . . Land is cheap here and everything grows good that is planted. . . . It is pretty warm and some fever but the fever is caused by the food they eat. At least I am willing to chance it. . . .We expect to be back at Concordia in about 1 month. Good luck to all you fellows.
>   J. P. Maxwell[9]

Around this time, according to Frank Aller, who had provided help for the earlier trouble in Chile, Sundance received his mail at the American Hotel in Oruro, Bolivia. Aller wrote in a letter that Sundance was known as "H. A. Brown or Frank Boyd. . . . I have a letter from him in which he stated that he would use the former name in Bolivia, in order to get 'honorable employment.'"[10]

As in the United States, many unsolved robberies were laid at the feet of Butch and Sundance. Most of the official information given by the police and newspapers came from the Pinkertons through Frank Dimaio. Articles appearing in newspapers in both the United States and in South America suggested at times that Sundance was the leader of the gang. The *New York Herald* and the *Denver Republican* each printed an article saying, "It is apparent that Longbaugh [*sic*], the leader of what is left of one of the most noted bands of robbers in this country."[11] Another article claimed, "Harry Longbaugh [*sic*] became the accepted leader of the outlaws." and referred to the gang as the *Sun-Dance Kids* and the *Sun Dance Gang.*[12]

In May 1908, two Americans stole the payroll from a railroad construction camp at Eucaliptus, Bolivia.[13] The thieves, who took 15,000 bolivianos, worth about $15,000, were thought to have been ex-employees of the railway. On August 19th the station was again robbed, and it was thought that the thieves were the same men as in the first robbery. Seibert claimed that Sundance and Butch were responsible for both holdups.

However, their participation at Eucalyptus is doubtful. By August 1908, both Sundance and Butch were working at the headquarters of A. G. Francis near Esmoraca, Bolivia. Francis was a British engineer employed by the San Juan del Oro Dredging Company and was supervising a gold dredge that was being moved on the river. Francis knew Sundance as Frank Smith and Butch as George Lowe; and he agreed to their request to bunk with his crew. What he didn't know was that they were there to plan a robbery.[14]

CHAPTER 29

Robbery of the Aramayo Mine Payroll

Sundance and Butch took shelter with Francis, who was moving a gold dredge on the San Juan del Oro River. While Sundance helped out around camp, Butch often traveled to Tupiza, a sizeable mining town about fifteen miles north of camp. He would spend a few days scouting out the local bank for a potential robbery and the possible escape routes before returning again to Francis's camp. In a few days, Butch would return to town again. Unknown to Francis, the outlaws had a problem. A local cavalry unit was also in town and had taken up residence in a hotel next door to the bank. So they waited and watched, and waited some more.

By late October, Sundance and Butch decided the job was too risky and changed their plans.[1] Butch had heard that an 80,000-peso payroll was being shipped by Aramayo Francke & Company, a mining enterprise which had an office in Tupiza. Both outlaws left camp and registered at the Hotel Terminus, from which they watched the Aramayo company office for signs of the payroll shipment.[2]

On November 3, 1908, Carlos Peró, the company manager, left the Aramayo office with his son Mariano and an employee named Gil Gonzalez.[3] They were trailing two pack mules and were headed for the mines at Quechisla, a rugged, three-day

journey. Butch and Sundance followed behind, their thoughts
on the 80,000 pesos and another attempt to go straight.

As Peró's group rested overnight at the village of Cotani,
Sundance and Butch quietly passed on ahead to Huaca Huañusca, in English, "Dead Cow." At the foot of a mountain
named for the shape of its spiny ridge, Huaca Huañusca was
a good site for an ambush. About 9:30 the next morning,
November 4th, Peró and the payroll escort rounded the bend
and found themselves facing Butch and Sundance who were
brandishing new, small-caliber Mauser carbines. They also
carried Colt revolvers, Browning pistols, and lots of rifle
ammunition, according to Peró's later reports. He described
the thieves as wearing dark red corduroy suits, with bandannas
pulled up over their faces, and hat brims turned down over
their eyes. Peró's note read:

> We encountered two well-armed Yankees, who awaited
> us with the faces covered by bandannas and their
> rifles ready, and they made us dismount and open the
> baggage, from which they took only the cash ship-
> ment. They also took from us a dark brown mule
> ("Aramayo"), which is known to the stable hands in
> Tupiza, with a new hemp rope.
> The two Yankees are tall; one thin and the other—
> who carried a good pair of Hertz binoculars—heavyset.
> They clearly came from Tupiza, where they must
> have been waiting for my departure to make their
> strike, because from the beginning they did not ask
> me for anything other than the cash shipment.[4]

Peró said that Sundance kept guard over them from a
distance and did not speak. Butch rode over to Peró and
demanded, in English, the 80,000-peso payroll. When Peró
replied that they were only carrying 15,000 pesos, amounting
to a little less than $100,000 today, Butch and Sundance were

clearly frustrated. The outlaws said that they did not want anything belonging to the men personally; instead, they commandeered one of the pack mules to carry the packet of money that was wrapped in homespun cloth.

Peró, his son, and Gonzalez were allowed to continue north with the second mule, and the outlaws headed south with the robbery proceeds toward Tupiza. Peró happened upon a muleteer, named Andrew Gutierrez, and quickly jotted down a note reporting the robbery. Gutierrez took the note back to Aramayo headquarters while Peró continued on to the mines without the payroll.

By the afternoon of November 4, 1908, nearly every town in the area had been alerted to the robbery and was watching for two strangers. Rather late that night, Sundance and Butch arrived in Tomahuaico, where dredging engineer A. G. Francis was currently camped. They awoke Francis and asked him for lodging; Butch appeared to be sick and went immediately to bed. Sundance, however, fixed himself something to eat and kept Francis up with tales of their latest heist.[5]

CHAPTER 30

San Vicente, Bolivia

After spending the night at the worksite with Francis, as they prepared breakfast, a mutual acquaintance rushed into camp to warn Francis, Sundance, and Butch that a military patrol from Tupiza was headed for Tomahuaico. At first Sundance and Butch seemed unconcerned—they leisurely finished breakfast and packed their horses. Then, however, they decided that Francis should accompany them as a guide toward Uyuni in the north. Francis felt more like a hostage. "Needless to say, that was the last thing I wished to do, but argument was useless. . . . Reflecting upon my position, I felt it to be a very unenviable one. . . . However, no other course being open to me, I decided to put as good a face on the matter as possible."[1]

The three men traveled as far as the Indian pueblo of Estarca, where they spent the night of November 5th. In the morning, Sundance and Butch thanked Francis and said goodbye, much to Francis's relief. They also said that if he should see any soldiers he should mention seeing the outlaws on the road headed south to Argentina. Sundance and Butch then continued on their way north. Although Francis believed they were heading for Uyuni, they were probably hoping to get to Oruro, where Sundance had recently been living in the American Hotel.

About sundown on the evening of November 6, 1908, Sundance and Butch arrived in the small mining village of San Vicente, Bolivia.[2] At 14,500 feet up in the Cordillera Occidental Mountains, it was definitely not the place to spend a night outdoors in the bitter cold and wind; above the tree line, the tundra was stark and without shelter. So they asked about overnight lodging at the home of Bonifacio Casasola, who referred them to Cleto Bellot, the town *corregidor*, a mayor or chief administrative officer. Bellot replied that there was no local inn but the men could stay with Casasola. When the men said they also wanted some sardines and beer, Bellot sent Casasola to purchase their supper with pesos that Sundance gave to him.

Bellot also left and immediately reported the pair of strangers to a military patrol that had arrived in town only a few hours earlier from Uyuni. The four-man patrol—Captain Justo P. Concha, Uyuni police inspector Timoteo Rios, soldier Victor Torres, and another unnamed soldier—was looking for the two Yankees who had stolen the Aramayo payroll and the company mule.

With Concha inexplicably absent—napping, drunk, or whatever—Torres took the lead, and the men entered Casasola's dark patio. Butch saw them and shot from the doorway, hitting Torres in the neck. Although mortally wounded, Torres was able to return fire as he backed out of the patio. The others retreated also but continued shooting from a safer distance. Bellot later reported hearing "three screams of desperation . . . no more shots were heard, except that the inspector [Rios] fired one shot at about midnight."[3]

After the initial gunfight was apparently over, Concha suddenly reappeared, and the patrol remained outside all night. The next morning, Casasola was sent into his house;

he immediately reported two dead bodies. The smaller outlaw (Butch) was stretched out on the floor, shot in the arm and in the temple. The larger of the two men (Sundance) was behind the door with his arms wrapped around a ceramic jar; he had several wounds in the arm and was shot in the forehead. Wounded, not wishing to rot in a Bolivian jail, or just clearly trapped, Butch had shot Sundance and then himself.

Although an inquest was held by the authorities in Tupiza, copies of that legal formality have not been found. There are, however, other reports and depositions that verify both the shootout and the apparent suicide deaths of the two Yankee bandits in the small town of San Vicente. A copy of the summary memorandum written on November 20th and signed by all who gave testimony was found. Cleto Bellot wrote, "This is to inform you that yesterday, at 3 P.M., a force from Uyuni commanded by Captain Justo P. Concha arrived in this vice canton with the aim of pursuing the robbers of the Aramayo, Francke and Company's cash shipment.

"The presumed robbers arrived here at about 7 P.M. Having been advised [of this fact], those in charge of the pursuit, in the company of the undersigned, presented themselves at the lodging of the men in order to identify them. We were fired upon, which caused a battle to be joined between the pursued and the pursuers, resulting in three dead—one soldier from the Uyuni column, Victor Torres, and the two foreigners, the alleged robbers."[4]

Remigio Sanchez, a miner from San Vicente, testified, "Two mounted gringos came from the east. . . . the police inspector, with two soldiers and the corregidor, immediately came to look and find out who the men were. . . . one of the gringos—the smaller one—appeared and fired one shot and then another from his revolver at the soldier. . . . he died in moments. . . . We remained all night until, at dawn, the captain ordered the owner of the house to go inside . . . and found the smaller gringo stretched out on the floor, dead, with one bullet wound in the temple and another in the arm. The taller one . . . was dead, also, with a bullet wound in the forehead and several in the arm."

Bellot further testified, "At about six in the morning, we were able to enter the room and found the two foreigners dead." A local magistrate by the name of Aristides Daza testified that he aided the authorities in a postmortem examination of the bodies. "I found a body in the threshold of Bonifacio Casasola's house with a revolver that appeared to have been fired . . . the other individual, who was on a bench, having used an earthen jug as a shield . . . finding him dead."

Daza proceeded to help inventory the personal effects of the two deceased outlaws. Sundance had, among other items, an 18-carat gold watch, no. 93,220, without crystal; a total of 93.50 bolivianos in his pocket; a dictionary; a new modified Winchester carbine, and 125 Winchester cartridges. In the luggage packed on the mules were a pair of binoculars, guns, more ammunition, and 14,400 bolivianos of Aramayo payroll money.[5]

The two deceased outlaws were buried in the San Vicente cemetery on November 7, 1908. For Sundance and Butch, the Outlaw Trail ended in San Vicente, Bolivia.

CHAPTER 31

Who Were Those Guys?

Born in the spring of 1867, Harry Alonzo Longabaugh died on November 6, 1908, at forty-one years old. His family did not acknowledge him for over sixty years; his sister Emma changed the spelling of the family name and disowned him when writing her will; and nearly three generations passed before his name was again mentioned by anyone in the family. He clearly broke the law, but others apparently remembered him in a better light.

In 1913, A. G. Francis recalled Sundance's death:

I must confess that it was with a feeling very much akin to grief that I wended my way home. [Sundance] told me once that he had made several attempts to settle down to a law-abiding life, but these attempts had always been frustrated by emissaries of the police and detective agencies getting on his track, and thus forcing him to the road. He claimed that he had never hurt or killed a man except in self-defense, and had never stolen from the poor, but only from rich corporations well able to support his "requisitions."

I certainly knew him as a most amiable and cheerful companion, possessed of a very equable temper.

> To conclude, I may mention that his favourite book
> was Rolf Boldrewood's 'Robbery Under Arms,' in which
> he greatly admired the character of "Old Man" Marston."[1]

Sundance apparently still enjoyed reading this book about the wilds of Australia.

On November 7, 1908, Francis happened to meet an Indian on the trail who told him that two white men had died in a shootout in San Vicente. Their description matched Sundance and Butch, the men he knew as Smith and Lowe. He learned a great deal about their last hours and in 1913 wrote an article titled "The End of an Outlaw" for *Wide World Magazine.* But his use of inaccurate, alias names clouded their true identities for many years.

Dan Gibbon, John Perry, and others living near Cholila already knew that their friends had died in Bolivia prior to 1911 when they gave depositions about Wilson and Evans, two other local outlaws. Fred Ings and Ebb Johnson, friends from far-away Canada, soon heard that Sundance and Butch had died; they both wrote memoirs during the 1930s in which they mentioned Sundance's death in South America.

Outlaw pals from the States also heard that Sundance and Butch were dead. Two friends, William Simpson and Matt Warner, claimed that men had been sent down to South America to verify their deaths. Warner also mentioned their deaths in a 1937 letter to author Charles Kelly as well as in his own 1939 autobiography. "[Butch] went to South America . . . and partnered with Harry Longabaugh. The two of 'em ranched and robbed in Bolivia and Argentina and was finally killed in a fight with soldiers that had been chasing 'em." As for their possible return to the States, Warner's opinion was, "It's all poppycock."[2]

When the two thieves were buried in San Vicente, they were buried as *desconocidos* or unknowns. This not only created a debate by historians that continues today but it was also an immediate problem back in Chile. On July 31, 1909, Frank D. Aller, the vice-consul from Antofagasta, wrote to the American minister at the American Legation in La Paz, Bolivia. Aller was trying to ascertain the identities of the two outlaws who died in San Vicente on November 6, 1908.

He wrote, "An American citizen named Frank Boyd is wanted in Antofagasta and letters addressed to him in Bolivia have failed to receive reply. . . . The last address of Frank Boyd or H. A. Brown was 'American Hotel,' Oruro. . . . I have been informed by Mr. Wm. Grey of Oruro, Mr. Thomas Mason of Uyuni and many others that Boyd and a companion named Maxwell or Brown were killed at San Vicente near Tupiza by natives and police and buried as 'desconocidos'. I have endeavored by correspondence to obtain confirmation and a certificate of death, but this has been impossible. . . . It is very important to locate Boyd alive, or failing this, to produce legal proof of his death. Everybody in Bolivia, except the authorities, seem convinced that the larger of the two men was Boyd and that possibly he had assumed the name of Brown."[3]

An interesting question is: why did Aller need to verify Sundance's death? Yes, to settle his estate. But who wanted to settle his estate? And what estate was there to settle? Was Ethel back in Chile trying to settle her husband's estate? Or was Sundance *wanted* in Antofagasta because of his earlier trouble with the Chilean authorities? Aller even stated that practically everyone believed Sundance was dead. "Everybody in Bolivia, except the authorities, seem convinced that the larger of the two men was Boyd [Sundance]."[4]

A follow-up to Aller's request was made by Alexander Benson of the American legation in La Paz, Bolivia. Benson wrote, "Legal proof of his [Sundance's] death is wanted by a Judge of the Court of Chile, in order to settle his estate."[5] Maybe Sundance had missed a court appearance or skipped out on his bail. Although much effort has been made to find evidence of such an estate or proceeding, nothing has yet come to light.

The Bolivian authorities' answer to Aller's request was, roughly translated, "I also submit to you the death certificates of the two said persons whose identifications are not known." Obviously that was not the answer he needed. On January 21, 1911, however, Aller received a second letter from the Bolivian authorities, who were "pleased to enclose herewith a complete record of the case of Maxwell and Brown, drawn up by the authorities of the district where they were killed."[6] Although no copy of that complete record apparently exists today, the letter does state that Maxwell and Brown were killed, and those were known to be the names used in Bolivia by Butch and Sundance, respectively.

In 1918, Emma Longabough, Sundance's sister, wrote a disclaimer in her will so as not to delay it being probated upon her death. In the will she stated, "whether my said brother Harry be living or dead, is not to change or affect this will." The family never officially heard of his death, but they believed that he had died somewhere in South America. Samanna's diary entries ended with her last letter to Sundance on April 22, 1905; all communication between them had ceased.

Finally, the general public heard about the deaths of Butch and Sundance in an article written by Arthur Chapman, "Butch Cassidy," in the April 1930 issue of *Elks Magazine*. Chapman's source for the article was Percy Seibert, of the Concordia tin mines. Seibert, who had personally known both Sundance and Butch, believed they had died in San Vicente.

In recent years, researchers Dan Buck and Anne Meadows have discovered many documents and local histories in South America that verify both the San Vicente shootout and the deaths of Butch and Sundance. In addition to the mound of evidence found by Buck and Meadows in South America, this author believes in the only statement ever made about Sundance by William H. Longabough, who was Sundance's nephew and this author's grandfather by marriage. Grand-pop once said, *I had an uncle who died in South America; he robbed banks and trains for a living and died in South America.*

Whatever Happened to Ethel?

Questions frequently arise concerning Ethel's true identity and fate. In a nutshell, no one really knows what happened to her. She disappeared as mysteriously as she came onto the scene. And, except for the six or seven years she spent with Sundance, very little is truly known about her.

Writer Horan's notes from his interviews with Percy Seibert read: "Eltel [*sic*] Place, ailing chronic appen. Sundance took her to Denver, went to cathouse, woke up alone, drunk fired, wanted coffee, got out town."[1] Thus began the story that she returned to the United States because of chronic appendicitis. While it seems impossible that someone with an attack of appendicitis would travel from South America to Denver for treatment—a long and arduous trip under healthy conditions—this presents one of the earliest explanations for her departure.

Because of the obvious difficulty in accepting this story, theory number two has her pregnant and wanting the child born at home in the United States. Either way, she reportedly returned to the States before she disappeared from history.

When Sundance and Butch originally sold their Cholila holdings in June of 1905, Sundance told their friends and employees that he was taking Ethel back to San Francisco. And the possibility of her return *alone* on board the S.S. *Seguranca* has been shown.

However, there is also some evidence that she returned with him, and lived in the port city of Antofagasta, Chile. The last sighting of her was reportedly on a raft crossing the Salado River while escaping shortly after the December 19, 1905, bank robbery in Villa Mercedes, Argentina.[2]

The only other reference to her was during the 1911 Wilson and Evans deposition, in the testimony given by Daniel Gibbon, who had been the ranch foreman at Cholila. He stated that Sundance told him she was living in San Francisco in 1906. If we accept that as an accurate statement, maybe she died along with six thousand other victims during the July earthquake and fires. Although her death would eliminate her from being the reason that Frank Aller was trying to settle Sundance's estate in 1909, we have seen some evidence that it was the authorities, not Ethel, who were trying to settle the estate.

A summary of the Argentine depositions taken in 1911 states that on their final trip out of the country Sundance and Ethel traveled under the name Mr. and Mrs. Matthews. Using this as a possible identity clue, together with the belief that she originally came from Texas, this author made a thorough search comparing Texas census records with California census records and San Francisco City directories.

In 1907, there was a listing for an E. Matthews living at 1417 San Bruno Avenue in San Francisco; but there was no indication as to the sex or full name of "E" Matthews. No Ethel Matthews appeared in the 1910 California census records. Because of the method in which California keeps marriage records, with both date and names required, no search for a possible second-marriage record was possible.

However, the search of Texas census and birth records did reveal a possibility. Ethel Angie Matthews was born October 3, 1877, to J. B. and S. E. Matthews in Morgan Mill, Erath

County, Texas. After the 1880 census record, there is no further local record of her. She filed a delayed birth record with the Social Security Administration on August 16, 1944, and a family member verified her information. But there was no mention of a married name for Ethel Angie Matthews, and she again disappeared. Although much easier to research than the California records, no marriage record has yet been found in Texas for Ethel Angie Matthews. For that matter, no marriage record has yet been found in Texas for anyone named Harry Longabaugh, Harry Alonzo, Harry Place, or Ethel Place.

Were Ethel Place, E. Matthews of San Francisco, and Ethel Angie Matthews the same person? Who knows. But that is currently our best lead and research continues.

Hangers-On and Wanna-Bes

No one ever claimed to be Ethel Place, although many researchers and writers have offered candidates over the years, this author included. For instance, Ethel Bishop, a woman living in a house of ill repute in San Antonio was a good possibility until her marriage certificate was found. The date definitely excluded her from being the true Ethel Place.

In spite of the large amount of evidence that has been found on the San Vicente, Bolivia, deaths of both Sundance and Butch, there have been numerous tales of their return for years. But, Jesse James, Billy the Kid, Elvis, and even John Lennon reportedly lived for decades after their announced deaths. It seems there are too many people who want to believe—that's why the con artist still succeeds.

Without death certificates after the San Vicente shoot-out, rumors surfaced to the effect that Butch Cassidy was still alive and again living in the United States. One Cassidy claimant was William Thadeus Phillips, who died in 1937 in Spokane, Washington. Although he never actually claimed to be Butch, he wrote a biography of Butch and his robberies that, to some readers, seemed too accurate for him not to be Butch.

However, over the last dozen years or so, evidence has been discovered that shows Phillips's mother was Celia Mudge of Sandusky, Michigan, and not Anne Gillies Parker of Utah. Phillips's own wife, Gertrude, denied any possibility of his being Butch, although she said the men had known each other.[1] In fact, the most recent possibility suggests that he was the Billy Phillips from Globe, Arizona, who testified in the murder trial of outlaw George Musgrave.[2]

In a 1983 book, Edward M. Kirby claimed that Hiram BeBee was the Sundance Kid.[3] BeBee, also known as George Hanlon, was a murderer who died at age eighty-eight in a Utah prison hospital on June 2, 1955. Kirby said that Sundance was not involved in any shootout in Bolivia, and he had therefore not died in 1908. Instead, he had returned to the United States to live out his life under a different and previously unknown name.

In facial features, BeBee looked more like comedian Jimmy Durante than the Sundance Kid. Furthermore, BeBee was nearly nine inches shorter than Sundance, and even osteoporosis doesn't shrink a person that much. Reported heights for Sundance show him from 5 feet 9 inches to 6 feet tall, while in 1919 BeBee was only 5 feet 2¾ inches tall, according to his prison records. And, although Kirby quoted BeBee's prison guard as saying that BeBee had boasted to fellow inmates about being Sundance, Kirby does not provide any record that BeBee ever made such a statement.

As noted above, Sundance died on November 6, 1908, in the village of San Vicente, Bolivia. Letters to family and friends ceased; old friends in Canada and the States heard that he had died; his neighbors in Cholila heard that he was dead; and records in South America provide too much circumstantial evidence to ignore. Magazine articles were written providing tidbits of proof; testimonies by those present at the shootout gave physical descriptions that match known descriptions of Sundance and Butch; and Aller was convinced that they were deceased.

Hiram BeBee had his fifteen minutes of fame; but he was definitely not Harry Alonzo Longabaugh, alias the Sundance Kid.

Shortly after the hit movie *Butch Cassidy and the Sundance Kid* was released in 1969, a man claiming to be Harry Longabaugh, Jr., began wandering throughout the West, giving interviews to local newspapers and lectures at area historical societies. Although he said that he was the son of the Sundance Kid, he never produced a birth certificate.[4]

In fact, he frequently changed, ever so slightly, the information he offered about his background. His birth name was either Harvey Longabaugh, Harry Thayne Longabaugh, or Harry Longabaugh II. He was born on either January 4 or February 2, 1901, in Cimarron, Texas; Cimarron, New Mexico; or Conconcully, Washington. He always claimed that his father was the Sundance Kid, and his mother was usually Anna Marie Thayne. Or maybe she was Mary Tryone, or Hazel Tryon Johnson Smith, or Etta (not Ethel) Place. He also said that Etta was a housewife from Castle Gate, Utah, who had deserted her two young children in order to follow Sundance to South America.

Because "Harry, Jr." made so many contradictory claims, none of which could be proven, people began to doubt his story entirely. He died on December 18, 1982, in Missoula, Montana, trying to escape from a fire in the Priess Hotel, where he was living. His so-called proof was apparently lost in the fire as well. His death certificate and county welfare funeral records list his name as Robert Harvey Longabaugh, born January 4, 1901, in Cimarron, New Mexico. His parents were Harold Longabaugh and Mary Tryone, and next of kin was a brother named John Harold Longabaugh

So, who was "Harry, Jr."? None of his story can be proved or disproved. But his photograph bears much too strong a family resemblance to Sundance for his story to be totally discredited. If he wasn't Sundance's son, maybe he was an unknown son of Elwood, Sundance's brother; or a son of Sundance's cousin, Seth Longabaugh.

Whoever he was, or whatever his legal name, our family believes that he was a Longabaugh.

Letters and News Articles

Many lengthy letters, newspaper articles, and Pinkerton files have been referred to or partially quoted within this book. And while the information has been important, it has often been too long to include entirely within the text. Therefore, some of the more pertinent pieces have been printed below, word for word, including grammar and spelling errors.

"Dad's Guest at the Old Slater Store"

David Gillespie's memorable meeting with mysterious strangers is here described by his son, David, Jr. The account, which accompanied the gift of his father's original letters on September 15, 1996, is part of the Gillespie papers at the Museum of North West Colorado, Craig.

In April 1896, twenty year old David Gillespie of Lincoln, Illinois, (my father) accompanied his uncle Hiram Parker of Lansing, Kansas, to the Little Snake River Valley where the uncle had some interests in gold mining. They did some placer gold mining that summer, but when Hiram returned to Kansas Dad stayed and accepted Robert McIntosh's offer to work at his Slater store and post office. Besides the store McIntosh had a livery stable and a building where meals and rooms were available. Dad who had bookkeeper and store-keeper experience in Illinois, worked at the McIntosh store from 1896 to 1904.

Dad considered a young cowboy who drifted into the Little Snake River Valley a good friend of his. This friend, Harry Lonzo, worked for A. R. Reader on the Savery Creek. He had a likeable personality and was an excellent bronc rider. By the time Harry left the valley, rumors were that he had been riding with the "Wild Bunch." Dad was one of those who didn't believe the rumors.

In a letter to his folks, dated October 12, 1897, Dad wrote: "I came very near going to Deadwood, South Dakota for a few days and it is barely possible that I may go yet. A young fellow a friend of mine who worked for Al Reader up till the middle of July left here near the first of August and went up there, and about the first of the month was arrested on the charge of having been in the bank robbery at that [p]lace on June 28. He was here at Slater on June 27 and up at Al's ranch on the 28th so couldn't possibly have taken part in the robbery. He fought the officers when they tried to arrest him and was shot in the arm and had his horse shot from under him. When arrested he didn't think it would amount to much so didn't give his right name and didn't want it to get into the papers. He and his lawyer both wrote here telling how the matter stood and wanted me and one or two others to go there to identify him and prove that he was on Snake River at the time of the bank holdup. Mr. McIntosh said that he could hardly spare me and if possible they had better get somebody else to go. Two left here last night so I think every-thing will be all right. I hope the fellow will get off all right for he is a mightly nice fellow. He is the best broncho rider around the country."

Later, (sometime between 1897 and 1901) as my dad told the story, late one evening after dark he was in the store catching up on some work when he heard a tap at the window. Going to the door he faced a stranger saying, "There's a man outside here who wants to see you." The stranger guided Dad to Harry Lonzo, Harry introduced the stranger to Dad, using a name that Dad did not recognize and could not later remember. Dad took meals to both of them and arranged a room for the stranger. Harry said to save money he would sleep in the livery stable.

That night, Lonzo went back into the store with Dad where the two of them visited for "quite a while," as Dad told. While visiting Harry paid Dad back money he'd borrowed from him, laying a gold coin on the counter and saying, "Keep the change." Dad questioned Harry, "Harry, there's a rumor you've been riding with the Wild Bunch. It isn't so, is it?"

Harry answered, "No, Dave, it isn't true."

The next morning the stranger ate breakfast upstairs at the table with several other men who had stayed there overnight. Dad took breakfast to Harry in the livery stable, then saw both of them off. As they were getting on their horses Harry said, "Dave, do you know this man?" Dad used the name that had been used for the stranger the night before. Harry answered, "He's Butch Cassidy."

Dad told the above story many, many times. Sometimes he would add, "I think that at the breakfast table that morning some of the men knew Cassidy but they never mentioned it."

Roy Letson's Letter to Charles Kelly

Roy Letson was an old-timer with firsthand knowledge to share with Charles Kelly, the author of The Outlaw Trail. *This letter can be found in Kelly's papers at the University of Utah, Salt Lake City.*

Dade City, Fla.
Jan 11th 1953

Dear Mr. Kelly:

Glad to learn from your letter of 1/1/53 that Jack Breed had sent you the letter which I wrote to him. When I read his article in National Geographic I was interested in his statement about Harry Longabough.

I still think if you could obtain a copy of the April 1930 issue of the Elk Magazine you would find it interesting.

I picked up Longabough in the Northern part of the Argentine 1907 while driving thru one hundred mules from the Argentine to LaPaz Bolivia for the Bolivian Government.

He was well dressed without funds, had a crust of bread in his pocket for his next meal.

He did have a fine Tiffany gold watch that his partner Butch Cassidy had purchased on his way thru New York City enroute to South America.

Longabough kept very much to himself most of the time.

I told him my destination was Bolivia and he said that he would be glad to go along.

We were several weeks on that trip. Traveling without any guide we would frequently come to a point where trails branched out in several directions. Longabough would suggest a trail & in each case he was correct. Shortly before reaching our destination & while sitting around a camp fire he told me that he knew every foot of the country & that he had been over the same trail many times.

He was employed by our company to break the mules to harness and saddle & done a very good job. Naturally he grew restless & it was not long before he was on the go again.

Longabough & Butch Cassidy robbed several camps & finally a good haul from one of the mining companies in Bolivia. While resting in one of the small outlaying towns they were surrounded by a group of soldiers. They fought for several hours & finally their ammunition almost completely gone (down to their last two shells) Butch Cassidy shot Longabough & then himself (I understand Longabough was very badly wounded at the time.)

Back in 1906 when I went to South America there were many who sought refuge in many of the countries there. No extradition laws between the US & South American countries in fact none between themselves. In meeting an American there very few questions were asked. I doubt if anyone knew of Longabough's past record.

Butch Cassidy while employed by one of the large mines there gave most of the story to one of the superintendents there & that's how the story in Elks Magazine came about.

I spent one year in South America & was paymaster on the construction job of the Bolivia Railway. We completed 150 miles of road & then our concession was sold to an English Syndicate who took over from there.

Most of our white help came to us from the States. Others who had worked in Panama, Ecuador, Peru & Chile.

Some came from South Africa & it was a common thing to sit down for a meal & no two could understand the other.

We had another character down there named Jack McVey from Brownsville Texas. Very little if anything was known of his record. He drifted to Brazil & so badly shot up there his friends got him back to Central America or some point near Brownsville where his folks could take care of him.

Another character was Dick Clifford. I think he was involved in some trouble around Chicago about 1904 or 5. I have not seen your book "Outlaw Trail" published in 1938. The 1930 (April) issue of Elks Magazine is in my possession—rather badly mutilated. If you fail to find a copy I will be glad to forward the one I have to you.

I am getting along in years. Will be seventy on my next birthday & I doubt if any of my heirs will be interested in any of my papers.

I spent a year 1919 to 1920 in Arizona. Liked it very much and bought property near Mesa (Apache Trail) which I sold in 1930. Came to Florida in 1931 & have never been out of the state.

Sincerely Roy Letson

The Standard (Buenos Aires), April 17, 1912

The Standard of Buenos Aires related the story of the Winnemucca (Nevada) bank robbery, as told by the Sundance Kid to an acquaintance in Argentina. Three years after the deaths of Sundance and Butch in Bolivia, the unnamed acquaintance wrote the account for this English-language newspaper in Buenos Aires. The article was discovered by British Wild Bunch researcher Michael Bell, who later wrote pieces comparing the many new finds with the few inaccuracies.

A short time ago there was published in these columns an article concerning the gang of outlawed desperadoes who having found their native health too sultry for them on account of the hue and cry raised by the misdeeds, came to this country for pastures new. The following story of one of their raids was told by one of the bunch to a gentleman at present residing here who has written it out for publication.

The Winnemocca Bank Hold Up,
as told by one of the Wild Bunch.

When the sheriffs of fourteen western states and Pinkerton Detectives read this title, they will put their ears to the ground and go off on a hot trail after yours truly.

So perhaps I had better get on the move, for I know those fellows and know they have a way of sticking to a trail once they have found it that makes a hunted man wish he hadn't done the act.

The Wild Bunch had dwindled to a handful, in fact you could count them all on one hand, out of a bunch of twenty hard hitting, straight shooting huskey cyclones that were in business only a few years ago, all were gone except a few of us; most of them went with their boots on; only one of the boys has an address that expires with himself.

My funds were getting low, so I drifted over to Powder Springs, Nevada; one of our numerous rendezvouses; where I hoped to find some of the bunch.

You bet I was glad to find two of the boys there on the same errand as myself.

After talking the matter over, we concluded to wait for our leader. Our Napoleon, the brainiest member of the bunch.

Days and dates cut no figure with us, summer and winter are the only periods of time that we take notice of.

So one bright sunny day in 1902 after loafing at the Springs for a month waiting for Harry Logan (Kid Curry), we started out to take in the Winnie Bank. The bunch consisted of Butch Cassidy, Geo Carver, and myself (Harry Lonbaugh [sic]). Carver was known to the man hunters as "Flat Nose George". We called him the Colonel, because he was such a large well proportioned man, with a military appearance, straight as an arrow and strong as a horse.

The boys sent me over to Winnemocca to size up the situation and pick out a trail for the get-away, while they went around to Twin Falls Idaho and bought horses.

I went down to Ogden where I caught a freight train one night and rode out on the bummers like a hobo and say; there was a Brakie on the train who used such vile and unsanitary language that it almost set my clothes afire, he finally made me jump off while the train was going twenty miles an hour, it would have been bad medicine for that brakie if I'd met him after the hold up.

One dark rainy night I arrived in Winnemucca, there were but few people on the streets, so without attracting much attention I made my way to a livery barn where I got permission to sleep on the hay pile, the next morning I got a job on the street, the shovel blistered my hands but I stuck to the job three days then quit, took my check for $7.50 to the bank to get it cashed and also to size up the interior decorations. Gee, but that sight was certainly good for sore eyes, it was the biggest little bank I had ever seen, the big stacks of yellow twenties looked so good and easy, that had I only had a horse hitched out in front the bank could have begun to lose out then and there.

While waiting for my turn at the window, I noticed a door in the back of the room. After getting my pay I went in again to see if the door was used often, or if it was kept locked during office hours, I had only a couple of hours to wait when I saw a man come out, when he went in again he used a key. About half a block down the alley west from the bank there was a vacant lot with a high board fence around it, just the place to leave our horses while collecting the legal tender. There was also a high wall around the back of the bank.

I had been in town three days, had the lay of the land down pat, the pay roll was certainly worth going after.

My work was finished and I was ready to go around to Twinn Falls and join the boys.

While on my way to the depot a man passed me and in the glance that he gave me I read recognition. No train for me after that look, it was cayuse or break into jail; so back to the barn I went, there I bought a pinto and saddle, I took the outfit to a pasture outside of town and paid for three days feed for the pony, then I went back to the hay loft and waited for darkness. I wrote a letter to the boys telling them to wait. After mailing the note I went back to the hay loft and jumped out the back door onto a manure pile, then I went to the pasture and stole my horse. It was about three hundred miles to Twin Falls, but I made it in six days. The cayuse was for sale when I arrived, but no one would have him as a gift. We went to Three Creek Post Office without incident, it was necessary to have grub cached at several different places along the trail for use on the way back from Winnemocca.

Having bought a lot of horses we were broke; we never stole a horse with which to make a raid, though on a get-away we took any kind that had good eyes.

Not having the cash to buy grub we had to hold up the store at Three Creek, the place was run by an old man and his wife. We called on them after they had gone to bed, the old man said he wouldn't trust us for a bill of goods, so we showed him our guns, after looking at the forty fives a half minute he said "Yes, I'll fill your order". We loaded two pack horses with grub and were about to leave when the old man said "Boys, I've got some good hats on the top shelf, perhaps you would like one apiece". Sure, we would. Butch and I got one each, but there was none large enough for the Colonel.

We rode into Winnemocca one morning before day-light and put our horses on the vacant lot. After eating breakfast that morning Butch and Colonel strolled about town. I kept out of sight for fear that some one would recognize me and give the alarm. About 9:30 Butch gave me the hurry up signal, when I crossed the street and met him he said, the sheriff is organizing a posse at the livery barn, so it's a chase for us now whether we take in the bank or not. The Colonel came up while we talking, he said it was suicide to attempt the hold up at that time, and advised postponing it for a month or so.

Butch said No; he said no futures for him, it was a case of run any way and he was going to do something to run for.

Alright said the Colonel, but here is where we get a per-manent address. We then went into the bank, Colonel had a rifle under his long coat he acted as doorkeeper. Butch car-ried the wad-bag to put the money in, my part was to do the scare act. I went to a window that had a sign over the top that read "Paying Teller". A nice pale looking man with his hair parted in the middle, asked "What can I do for you Sir", "Hand over the money I answered", at the same time pulling a pair of Forty Five Colts on him, "Up with your hands" I said "stick 'em up everybody". There was a tall slim sallow faced kid working at a typewriter over in the corner. He didn't hear me at first, then I yelled at him "stick 'em up slim or I'll make you look like a naval target."

When the poor fellow turned and saw what was going on he collapsed, he put his hands up but couldn't keep them there. Anybody that wished to come into the bank, Colonel made them join the row of high reachers that stood against the wall. Butch went down the corridor and through a gate in the wire fence. He had just got inside the corral, when a man came out of the back room; Butch greeted him with a smile and said "Friend my associates would like to speak to you at the teller's window."

When he had gotten into line of my forty five he said "What is going on here? what does this mean?" "It grieves me to inform you that the bank is losing out" replied Butch who was then transferring the pay streak to the wad bag. "Say friend" I said to the late arrival "Just feel how soft and fine the atmosphere is above your head, feel it with both hands at once". They were all up, and nobody made a move while Butch went into the vault and filled the wadbag with gold coin.

The job was done and we were starting away when the paying teller said "Boys you have a nice little stake there, but I don't think you will be able to hold onto it". "Think again" replied Colonel as we went out the door and fastened it behind us.

We went out the back way and when I got to the top of the wall I saw the posse lining up in front of the bank. Butch passed the wadbag to me and just as I was about to drop it to the ground a man with a gun came to the mouth of the alley, he was about as mean a looking specimen as I have ever seen, he looked like some pictures I've seen of the Western Bad man, he had a long black mustache, and eyebrows almost as long as the mustache.

"There's a gun fighter" I called to Butch "get him quick". Colonel jumped on the wall and fired, tearing up the dirt in front of the bad man who threw down his gun and ran away. We ran to the horses. Butch had a fine bay mare and as he was the lightest man I handed him the sack.

We had to go out on the main street in order to hit the trail towards the east. Away we went, Colonel in the lead and I bringing up the rear. The posse evidently intended to hold an informal reception in front of the bank with the wild bunch as entertainers.

They were lined up in a brave array behind boxes, barrels and brick piles that stood along the main street. So when we went out onto the street two blocks east, their breast works were of no use, we had an open trail ahead and only a few more blocks to go, then we would be out in open country, with nobody in front to stop us, when "great balls of cod fish hooks," Butch dropped the wadbag, which bursted when it dropped to the ground. The bay mare seemed to go straight up when she lost the weight.

Colonel was two hundred yards away before he knew that something was wrong, then he wheeled round and came back.

While Butch and I was scraping up the yellow boys and putting them in a new sack, Colonel smoked the posse out of sight with a 30 U.S.

After making the bag fast to the saddle we hit the sand again, leaving five or six thousand dollars in the street.

As we raced along, faces were peeping from windows like owls from hedge rows. The train ran along side of the railroad a mile and a half to a place where we had fresh horses and more guns cached.

We hadn't gone far before we saw we were up against something we hadn't counted on. Chased by a locomotive—who'd thought of that.

On it came, the engineer had it wide open and the fireman was doing his damnedest; I could tell that by the roll of smoke that was belching from the stack.

We were about half way to our fresh horses when the engine got in range.

At the first volley my old roan was shot in the belly. I was about fifty yards behind Butch, who kept banging away with his forty-five. My horse began to lose ground. I emptied my gun once and had put in a fresh round. The engine was within twenty yards of me; the bullets were flying thick, the air seemed to be sizzling with the hot lead when the Colonel got into the game, he was a good shot and that crew soon found it out. He began pumping lead straight at the cab. I could see the splinters fly with every shot; finally one of his shots broke a steam pipe somewhere, then nothing could be seen of the engine but a black front, the cab was a fog bank. The moving fort was put out of commission or they would have gotten me, for I had to walk the last hundred yards and carry my saddle.

We had eight horses at the cache, two of them were pack horses, so we tied the wadbag onto a pack saddle and started for the hole in the wall. We had some good horses and rode them to their limit of speed until daylight next morning when we came to a ranch where we had left five of the best horses that we could find in Idaho, but say—if you want to get good longwinded race horses go to Winnemocca, they've got them there, or at least they had some once upon a time.

That posse was on to us before we had time to change mounts; they didn't give us time to eat, we had to smoke them back while we finished changing our outfit.

I am sure we had ten miles start of the bunch when they left Winnemocca and we had changed mounts several times during the night. How did the posse keep on our trail?

There they were anyway, but with tired horses. They chased us across the pasture, we cut the wire fence and went out into the open about three hundred yards ahead of them.

We rode like blazes until noon then stopped for lunch. Butch had just built a fire and put on the coffee pot while I had open a couple of cans of Three Creek meat when Colonel, who was on guard, shouted "Here they come again and they're coming some too."

One look at the posse was enough to make us bust a hole in the atmosphere again, for them fellows back there was sure burning the breeze.

Away we went, not in a canter, but as hard as we could ride. The posse gained on us steadily. We were nearing the southern foothills of Bruneau Mountain; if we could only make timber line we were safe. All afternoon we rode, with the posse sometimes within a quarter of a mile of us. About 5 p.m. we saw a small grove ahead. There we was going to make a stand, but as we neared the timber we saw the posse spreading out and knew that to stop meant surrounded, so we just trotted through the grove and down into a gulch, which we followed for a mile before the posse discovered that they had only surrounded our tracks.

We were not in rough country, a tired horse is no good at hill climbing, so we got off and walked, driving the horses ahead. We kept out of range of the posse till dark, then we were safe from pursuit, for the hills were rocky and it would be a hard matter to track us in daylight and in the dark impossible.

Since striking the hills, we had been going due north towards a pass at the head of Jaybridge canyon. When we were sure that we had shaken the posse, we turned east and traveled east as fast as the tired horses could go for three hours then we camped—"Hungry, tired" well, I should say we were all about dead.

Thirty-six hours in the saddle, riding as only a hunted man can ride, and all the while nothing to eat, and to add to our misery it began to rain. It is always cold up in that mountain at night. I would have given a hat full of that coin for a cup of hot coffee, but we dared not make a fire. We ate a lot of the old man's canned stuff, then we took two hours turn on guard. Colonel went on first and when he came off and tried to wake Butch he made so much noise that I woke up and went on guard. It was a long two hours; once I went to sleep standing up. I fell down and skinned my face, that kept me awake for the balance of my watch. I went and tried to wake Butch. I kicked him in the ribs, I pulled his hair, not a move out of him; then I whispered in his ear "They're coming". It was like magic, Butch was on his feet in a flash and I heard the forty five click as he came up. "Where at" he asked. "About fifteen miles west", I replied. "And you stand over there under that tree a couple of hours and call us when they closer".

I then turned in for four hours sleep with the cold drizzle still falling. How was the posse faring? Much better, for they could make a fire and make a lot of noise cutting branches for a shelter. Their number was being constantly recruited with fresh men and horses, while we would still have forty miles to go before we could get fresh mounts.

We traveled all day, up the gulch we had camped on the night before. It lead to the pass we were trying to make.

We were within two miles of the pass when Colonel, who had went ahead to look for signs, gave us the stop signal. We went up and peeped over the ridge; we saw twenty-five men riding slowly towards the pass.

We doubled back to our last camp and made a fire, cooked some grub, boiled coffee and had a feast.

We went around the mountain and into Idaho by an east side pass, coming out at the head of Three Creek.

Down a little gulch where there was horse feed we divided the cleanup and as the pack horses were played out and we get to the cache in Jabridge, we concluded to bury the money there, each man to plant his own separate and not let the others know where he put it.

Colonel put six thousand five hundred dollars in an empty lard pail and went down the gulch. I put my share in the wadbag and went up stream, leaving Butch in camp.

As I was returning after hiding the coin I saw Colonel on top of a hill above the trail. When he joined us again he seemed to have gotten a hunch for he started to tell where he had hidden his pile. "Shut up" I said, "We don't want to know where it is. Some one may lift it then you could blame us."

We sat down and figured up the old man's grocery bill for groceries and hats, then doubled the amount and put it in a sack, which we left at the store as we passed that night.

We had three days' peace and rode slowly to Snake River. There the chase took on so much new life that it made the first edition look like a cake walk.

Once we were fifty-two hours in the saddle; up through Idaho and on into Wyoming we went, with a posse in sight every day. We were making for a small lake in hole in the wall. Colonel knew the place, Butch and I didn't.

We were trying to get grub enough to last three months, as we intended to keep under cover that long. Colonel had gone to a camp wagon by himself while Butch and I tackled another. We had gotten all the grub that our horses could carry and was riding away with it when we saw a horseman riding along the opposite ridge; he was riding for first money; he sure was getting some speed out of that big bay horse. That was the last we ever saw of Colonel. It was him—he had sighted the posse.

Butch and I cut the grub adrift and hit a course to the east. The man hunters never let up. They drove us across the red desert and into Utah, into Nevada and back into Idaho, then we shook them and went over to Powder Springs to wait for Colonel, as he knew that we could not make our way to the lake.

We remained at the springs three weeks and were making preparations to leave one evening, when a posse came onto us unexpectedly, both sides were taken by surprise. There was a savage gun fight that lasted about five minutes.

We made a get away without horses and went back and dug up the money, still not knowing that jolly, big hearted kind old Colonel had cashed in. The posse got him. The law had chased us two thousand miles on horse back and during the trip we used up one hundred and twenty two horses, we suffered hardships to the limit of endurance.

We had lost a comrade that we loved like a brother. Now if you ask "Is the pay worth the work?" I would say "No" but it is a game that once you button into, the law won't let you break away from, unless you go to jail.

One day Colonel told Butch where he had buried his money. It is there yet, on top of a hill about four miles from Three Creek, Idaho. I wouldn't go back after it if it was multiplied by ten thousand.

The Daily Yellowstone Journal, June 7 and 9, 1887

On June 7, 1887, the Daily Yellowstone Journal *of Miles City, Montana, published a front-page article about the original arrest and escape of young Harry Longabaugh after the robbery on the Three V Ranch. The article further mentioned his second arrest and credited him with nearly every robbery in the area during the intervening weeks; they then compared him with the outlaw Jesse James.*

He Played 'Possum

How Deputy Sheriff E. K. Davis
Fooled a Fly Young Criminal
He had in Charge

The Astonishing Record of Crime
Perpetrated by Harry Longabaugh
In Three Weeks

A Fly Kid
And the Way He was Caught Up by
Officers Davis and Smith

On Saturday Deputy Sheriff Davis, together with Stock Inspector Smith, made a most important arrest. It will be remembered that about a month ago Harry Longabaugh, a criminal wanted in Sundance, and who was arrested by the officers here and turned over to Sheriff Ryan of Crook county, Wyoming, escaped from the train while in motion, in Minnesota, Sheriff Ryan being there in performance of his duty in taking him back to Wyoming soil. The kid had not been heard of till very lately, and was arrested as above stated by Deputy Davis near the N-bar ranch on Powder river.

After his escape from Sheriff Ryan he made his way back to Montana over the Canadian Pacific, and just before leaving Canadian soil stole seven head of horses from an operator on the new road and sold them near Benton. He came south and stopped at Billings three days and from there went to the Crow reservation, where he stole a pony, which is now in possession of Sheriff Irvine. He perpetrated the robbery of the FUF ranch, which was detailed in these columns a few days ago, and from there proceeded to Beasley & Newman's sheep ranch and stole a horse from P.G. Wear. He it was who stole and cut the saddles at Kirwan & Langley's ranch on Tongue river, and he stole a horse from Geo. Liscom's ranch on the same river. He planned to get away with a bunch of twelve mares belonging to Liscom, but slipped up on that for some reason. The rest of his planned expeditions were nipped in the bud by his arrest.

After Mr. Davis had made the arrest he took three six-shooters from the bold young criminal and shackled him and handcuffed him with some patent lock bracelets which were warranted to hold anything until unlocked by the key and which the manufacturers offered a premium if they could be opened otherwise. Eph Davis had heard a good deal of Longabaugh's prowess in effecting escape, and after taking all due precautions when night closed in upon them he lay down in one corner of a shack and Mr. Smith another, the kid between them. Smith was tired out and soon fell to sleep and Davis played 'possum, keeping an eye on the prisoner. Soon as he thought everyone was asleep the kid, shackled and manacled as he was, managed to free himself and rising stealthily approached the window and raised it and was about to make a break for liberty when sly old Eph thought it was time for him to take a hand and raising on his elbow with a cocked six-shooter in his hand he said in a quiet tone of voice, "Kid, your loose, ain't you?" and then called to Smith. The kid dropped back as though he was shot and it is needless to add that the officers did not sleep at the same time during the rest of the night.

Resolving not to lose his prisoner or reward this time, Sheriff Irvine has telegraphed Sheriff Ryan asking what he will give for the Kid laid down in Sundance. Talk about the James boys, this fellow has all the necessary accomplishments to outshine them and Tom Irvine considers him one of the most daring and desperate criminals he has ever had to deal with. The stretch of country he has covered in a short time and the success of all his planned robbery was almost phenomenal. Deputy Davis and Inspector Smith did a mighty good job when they nailed the Kid without some blood being spilt. He acknowledged himself done up when landed in this jail and expresses much admiration for our officers in the way they did the business.[4]

Taking offense at the extent of the accusations, Harry wrote a letter to the editor of the Daily Yellowstone Journal, *which published his response on June 9, 1887.*

In your issue of the 7th inst. I read a very sensational and partly untrue article, which places me before the public not even second to the notorious Jesse James. Admitting that I have done wrong and expecting to be dealt with according to law and not by false reports from parties who should blush with shame to make them, I ask a little of your space to set my case before the public in a true light. In the first place I have always worked for an honest living; was employed last summer by one of the best outfits in Montana and don't think they can say aught against me, but having got discharged last winter I went to the Black Hills to seek employment— which I could not get—and was forced to work for my board a month and a half, rather than to beg or steal. I finally started back to the vicinity of Miles City, as it was spring, to get employment on the range and was arrested at the above named place and charged with having stolen a horse at Sundance, where I was being taken by Sheriff Ryan, whom I escaped from by jumping from the cars, which I judged were running at the rate of 100 miles an hour.

After this my course of outlawry commenced, and I suffered terribly for the want of food in the hope of getting back south without being detected, where I would be looked upon as I always had been, and not as a criminal. Contrary to the statement in the Journal, I deny having stolen any horses in Canada and selling them near Benton, or anyplace else, up to the time I was captured, at which time I was riding a horse which I bought and paid for, nor had I the slightest idea of stealing any horses. I am aware that some of your readers will say my statement should be taken for what it is worth, on account of the hard name which has been forced upon me, nevertheless it is true. As for my recapture by Deputy Sheriff Davis, all I can say is that he did his work well and were it not for his "playing 'possum" I would now be on my way south, where I had hoped to go and live a better life.

Harry Longabaugh

Pardon Granted

On February 4, 1889, Wyoming's Governor Thomas Moonlight signed a full pardon for Harry Longabaugh. There is no evidence that Sundance actually received the pardon before his release from jail. The pardon is in the Court Archives of Crook County, Wyoming. A copy is in the author's possession.

"Whereas, Harry Longabaugh was at the August, 1887 term of the District Court within and for the County of Crook convicted of the crime of Grand Larceny and sentenced by said Court to a term of eighteen months in the penitentiary being County Jail of Crook County. His term of sentence will expire Feb. 5, 1889; that he is still under 21 years of age, and his behavior has been good since confinement, showing an earnest desire to reform and whereas the sheriff, Clerk of Dist. Court, Ex. Co & Pros. Attorney and present Co. & Pros. Atty. And others have this day made application to me to grant unto the said Harry Longabaugh a pardon of said crime of which he stands convicted.

Therefore, by the authority vested in me as Governor of the Territory of Wyoming, I do hereby grant unto Harry Longabaugh a full and complete pardon of the crime of which he was convicted and hereby restore him to all of his civil rights.

In Testimony whereof I have hereunto set my hand and caused to be affixed the great seal of the Territory of Wyoming, at Cheyenne, this fourth day of February 1889.

Butch Cassidy Letter from Cholila, Argentina

This is the first page of a letter written by Butch to the mother-in-law of his friend Elzy Lay. The remainder of the letter and closing signature are missing.

Cholila, Chubut
Argentine Republic, S. Am.
August 10, 1902

Mrs. Davis
Ashley, Utah

My dear friend,

I suppose you have thought long before this that I had forgotten you (or was dead) but my dear friend I am still alive, and when I think of my Old friends you are always the first to come to my mind. It will probably surprise you to hear from me away down in this country, but U. S. was too small for me. The last two years I was there, I was restless. I wanted to see more of the world. I had seen all of the U. S. that I thought was good, and a few months after I sent A——over to see you; and get the Photo of the rope jumping of which I have got here and often look at and wish I could see the originals, and I think I could liven some of the characters up a little, for Maudie looks very sad to me. Another of my uncles died and left $30,000, Thirty Thousand, to our little family of 3, so I took my $10,000 and started to see a little more of the world. I visited the best Cities and best parts of the countrys of South A. till I got here, and this part of the country looked so good that I located, and I think for good, for I like the place better every day. I have 300 cattle, 1500 sheep, and 28 good Saddle horses, 2 men to do my work, also good 4-room house, wearhouse, stable, chicken house and some chickens. The only thing lacking is a cook, for I am still living in Single Cussedness and I sometimes feel very lonely, for I am alone all day, and my neighbors don't amount to anything, besides, the only language spoken in this country is Spanish, and I don't speak it well enough yet to converse on the latest scandals so dear to the hearts of all nations, and without which conversations are very stale, but the country is first class. The only industry at present is stock raising (that is in this part) and it can't be beat for that purpose, for I have never seen a finer grass country, and lots of it hundreds and hundreds of miles that is unsettled and comparatively unknown, and where I am it is a good agricultural country. All kind of small grain and vegetables grow without Irrigation, but I am at the foot of the Andes Mountains, and all the land east of here is prairie and Deserts, very good for stock, but for farming it would have to be irrigated, but there is plenty of good land along the Mountains for all the people that will be here for the next hundred years, for I am a long way from Civilization. It is 16 hundred miles to Buenos Aires, the Capital of Argentine, and over 400 miles to the nearest Rail Road or Sea Port in the Argentine Republic, but only about 150 miles to the Pacific Coast Chile, but to get there we have to cross the mountains, which was thought impossible till last summer, when it was found that the Chilean Gov. had cut a road almost across, so that next summer will be able to go to Port Mont, Chile, in about 4 days, where it use to take 2 months around the old trail, and it will be a great benefit to us for Chile is our Beef market and we can get our cattle there in 1/10 the time and have them fat. And we can also get supplies in Chile for one third what they cost here. The climate here is a great deal milder than Ashley Valley. The summers are beautiful, never as warm as there. And grass knee high everywhere and lots of good cold mountain water, but the winters are very wet and disagreeable, for it rains most of the time, but sometimes we have lots of snow, but it don't last long, for it never gets cold enough to freeze much. I have never seen Ice one inch thick.

Notes

Chapter 2. The Early Years

1. Family Records; 1840, 1850, 1860, and 1870 U.S. Federal Census Records, Pennsylvania; local annual head tax records, Montgomery County, Pennsylvania; Donna B. Ernst, *Sundance, My Uncle,* 10–20, hereafter referred to as *SMU;* the various spellings of each branch of the Longabaugh family have been carefully adhered to.

2. German Indentured Servants records, Pennsylvania; Rupp, *Immigrants in Pennsylvania,* 404, and *Pennsylvania German Pioneers,* Vol. I, 744–45. Conrad's indenture was held by John Hunter of Chester County, Pennsylvania.

3. Family Bible; 1870 and 1880 U.S. Federal Census Records, Pennsylvania.

4. Local head tax records, and family records.

5. U.S. Government Pension records and Army discharge papers.

6. Local head tax records; the house was located on the Schuylkill Canal, and Josiah was working with his brother Michael on the canal boats at the time. The house burned down in 1999.

7. Pennypacker, *Annals of Phoenixville,* 164–69, 222.

8. Ibid., 169–70, 226.

9. 1880 U.S. Census records, Chester County, Pennsylvania; *SMU,* 20.

10. Whaling Ship records; Pinkerton Report dated April 23, 1902; the Pinkerton Archives contain many addresses for the Longabaugh siblings.

11. *SMU*, 96–99.

12. Pinkerton Detective Agency Archives, Library of Congress, Washington, D.C., hereafter referred to as *Pinkertons*.

13. Ibid., memo dated Nov. 17, 1921, signed by Wm. A. Pinkerton.

14. Ibid., binder 6, p. 7.

15. Siringo, *Cowboy Detective*, 361.

16. Family records; author's correspondence and interviews with family members.

17. The Longabaugh family lived at 354 Church Street in Phoenixville. Local head tax records, Phoenixville City Directory, and family records.

18. Correspondence and interviews with descendants of George Longenbaugh; *SMU*, 10–20.

Chapter 3. Ranching in Cortez, Colorado

1. Correspondence and interviews with descendants of George Longenbaugh; *SMU*, 23–30.

2. *SMU*, 23–30; Deer Lodge State Prison records, Montana Historical Society, Helena, Montana.

3. Correspondence and interviews with descendants of George Longenbaugh; *SMU*, 23–30.

4. Jessen, *Colorado Gunsmoke*, 247; *Rocky Mountain News*, June 27, 1889; *SMU*, 55.

5. Baker, *Wild Bunch at Robbers Roost*, 57–58; Warner, *Last of the Bandit Riders*, 110–16; *SMU*, 29–30.

6. Baker, Wild Bunch at Robbers Roost, 110–13; *SMU*, 25–30.

Chapter 4. The Outlaw Trail

1. Gatchell, "Hole in the Wall," *Annals of Wyoming*, 1958.

2. Tennent, *John Jarvie of Brown's Park*, 65–69; Kouris, *History of Brown's Park*, 77–78; *Denver Post*, November 20, 1977; and SMU, 66–71.

3. Willis, "Queen Ann"; Kouris, *History of Brown's Park*, 78.

4. BLM Homestead Records at www.glorecords.blm.gov show Matt's eighty-acre homestead was located in Sweetwater County, Wyoming, in Township 12 north and Range 97 west. Building foundations can still be seen on this privately owned ranch.

5. *Craig Courier*, January 16, 1897; John F. Gooldy memoirs.

6. Warner, *Last of the Bandit Riders*, 136–43; *SMU*, 69–71.

7. *From Buffalo Bones to Sonic Boom*, 6; Segars, *100 Years in Culbertson*, 127.

8. J. D. B. Grieg letter to Pinkerton Detective Agency, *Pinkertons*; Brekke, *Kid Curry*, 50, 52, 56; *SMU*, 36.

9. French, *Recollections*, 251–83; *SMU*, 70–71.

10. Siringo, *Cowboy Detective*, 354; and French, *Recollections*, 272–73.

Chapter 5. The Suffolk Cattle Company

1. John B. Thomas Papers.

2. Sam W. Mather of Eldorado, Texas, in letter dated August 27, 1928, to *Frontier Times* (published in October 1928).

Chapter 6. The N Bar N Ranch

1. Information compiled from Lee I. Niedringhaus, *The N Bar N Ranch*, 1–32; *SMU*, 31–37; *From Buffalo Bones*, 5–6; *Brand Book of the Montana Stock Growers Association for 1885 and 1886*, 16 and 91.

2. Letter to editor of *Daily Yellowstone Journal* (Miles City, Montana), June 9, 1887, Harry wrote in response to an earlier news commentary of his misdeeds.

Chapter 7. Robbery on the Three V Ranch

1. Garman, "Harry Longabaugh," 6; *SMU*, 38–47.

2. *Sundance Gazette*, March 18, 1887; Crook County Wyoming Court Records.

3. *Sundance Gazette*, April 8, 1887.

4. *Centennial Roundup*, 1987; *Miles City (Mont.) Star*, 43.

5. *Daily Yellowstone Journal*, April 12, 1887.

6. *Sundance Gazette*, April 22, 1887.

7. Pointer, *In Search of Butch Cassidy*, 48; Patterson, *Historical Atlas of the Outlaw West*, 98.

8. James D. Horan notes, taken during interview with Percy Seibert, state in part "Sundance—slim wrists—slipped cuffs," in Robert G. McCubbin Collection.

9. (*Miles City*) *Big Horn Sentinel*, June 11, 1887; and *Miles City Daily Gazette*, June 8, 1887.

10. *Daily Yellowstone Journal,* June 9, 1887.

11. Ibid., June 7, 1887.

12. Ibid., June 9, 1887.

13. *Sundance Gazette,* June 24, 1887.

14. *Daily Yellowstone Journal,* June 21, 1887.

15. Garman, "Harry Longabaugh," 4; family records, and Crook County (Wyoming) Court Records.

Chapter 8. The "Kid" Gets a New Name

1. *Sundance Gazette,* July 22, 1887.

2. Indictments found in the records of Clerk of the Court Office, Crook County Courthouse, Sundance, Wyoming.

3. Court records provided at Crook County Courthouse, Sundance, Wyoming. Because the transcript of his appearance is actually missing, this was quoted by H. R. Bernd and placed in the court files.

4. Garman, "Harry Longabaugh," 4–5.

5. *Sundance Gazette,* May 4, 1888.

6. Records of Charities and Reform, Minutes of the Penitentiary Commission, as found in Garman, "Harry Longabaugh," 5.

7. Copy of Pardon in author's possession.

8. *Sundance Gazette,* February 8, 1889.

9. Ibid., May 17, 1889.

10. Arrest warrant, Crook County Court Records, Sundance, Wyoming; *SMU,* 39–47.

Chapter 9. Telluride Bank Robbery

1. *Rocky Mountain News,* June 27, 1889; *Pueblo Chieftain,* June 26, 1889, mentions that a fourth man held the horses; *SMU,* pages 48–55; and interviews by author with descendants of George Longenbaugh.

2. Baker, *Wild Bunch at Robbers Roost,* 161–63; McCarty, *Own Story,* 29.

3. Copy of 1971 C. M. Engel letter to Walter Longenbaugh, in author's possession.

4. Jessen, Colorado Gunsmoke, 247; *Rocky Mountain News,* June 27, 1889; Warner, *Last of the Bandi Riders,* 117–23; McCarty, *Own Story,* 26–29, 54; Patterson, *Butch Cassidy,* 21–31; *SMU,* 48–55.

Chapter 10. A Cowboy in Calgary

1. Interviews with the Johnson family; Ebb Johnson, unpub. memoirs; Donna B. Ernst, "Sundance, The Missing Years," 20–23.

2. *Leaves from the Medicine Tree*, 257, 368; Bert Sheppard, "Just about Nothing," 76–77.

3. Ings, *Before the Fences*, 41–53, 151–54; Ernst, "The Missing Years," 20–23.

4. Copy of Canadian government census records in author's possession.

5. The marriage certificate is still in the possession of Johnson's descendants today. The family also recalls that in later years Sundance made a number of visits while escaping the law in the States.

6. Ings, *Before the Fences*, 41–53.

Chapter 11. Train Robbery in Malta

1. Robbery details are compiled from the *River Press* (Malta, Mont.), November 30 and December 7, 1892; *Chinook (Mont.) Opinion,* December 1 and 8, 1892; *Great Falls (Mont.) Daily Tribune,* November 30, 1892; and *SMU,* 79–83.

2. Montana State Archives and Historical Society, Helena, Montana.

3. *Great Falls Tribune,* December 1, 1892.

4. Interviews with John G. Lepley and John Witt of the River & Plains Society, Ft. Benton, Montana.

5. *Great Falls Tribune,* December 8, 1892.

6. Ibid.

7. *Pinkertons,* cipher list.

8. *From Buffalo Bones,* 5–6.

Chapter 12. The Little Snake River Valley

1. Donna B. Ernst, "Wyoming Cowboy," 17; Donna B. Ernst, "Friends of the Pinkertons," 34–36; Donna B. Ernst, "Snake River Valley and the Sundance Kid," 6–8; John F. Gooldy memoirs; David Gillespie, letters.

2. Correspondence and interviews with Jean Beeler Russell of Dixon, Wyoming.

3. Oliver St. Louis interview on file at Museum of North West Colorado, Craig, Colorado.

4. Gooldy memoirs.

5. Ibid.

6. Interviews and letters from Ed Wren, grandson of Ed Wren; Gooldy, memoirs.

7. *Pinkertons*, cipher list.

8. Ayers eventually purchased the Two Bar and re-named it the L 7 Ranch.

9. *Pinkertons*, ID card for Sundance, written by Charlie Ayers, in Sundance Kid file.

10. The rifle is still owned by the Leahy family today; Ed Wren interview.

11. *Craig Courier,* January 9, 1897.

12. Ibid., January 16, 1897.

Chapter 13. Belle Fourche Bank Robbery

1. Details are compiled from the *Pioneer Times* (Black Hills), June 29, 1897; the *Sundance Gazette,* July 2, 1897; court testimony and records concerning robbery provided by Doug Engebretson of Belle Fourche, South Dakota; *SMU,* 84–95; Engebretson, *Empty Saddles,* 171–81.

2. *Billings Gazette,* September 28, 1897.

3. Gillespie, letters.

Chapter 14. Capture and Escape

1. *Rawlins Republican,* July 30, 1897.

2. Ibid.

3. *Billings Times,* September 30, 1897; *SMU,* 89–95. A recently found photograph appears to show Sundance, Punteney, and Logan walking in chains down a street in Billings. Efforts to verify have not yet been successful.

4. *Billings Gazette,* September 24 and 28, 1897; other robbery details are compiled from the *Billings Times,* September 30, 1897; *Sturgis Weekly Record,* October 1, 1897; *Queen City Mail of Belle Fourche,* September 29, 1897; Donna B. Ernst, "Butte County Bank Holdup," 35–37; and Donna B. Ernst, "A Deadwood Jail Break," 13–15.

5. *Billings Gazette,* September 24, 1897.

6. Gillespie, letters.

7. Ibid.

8. *Daily Pioneer Times,* October 2, 1897.

9. Goodly memoirs; Gillespie, letters; and court records from Lawrence County, South Dakota.

10. *Pinkertons,* a series of letters to and from Frank Hadsell, dated Feb. 13 and 20, Mar. 6 and 10, and Nov. 19, 1901, and Pinkerton agent Frank Murray.

11. McCoy, *Tim McCoy Remembers the West,* 67–71, 80; Donna B. Ernst "Walt Punteney and Tom O'Day," 18–20, 72.

12. Frank P. Hadsell's files, Wyoming State Archives, Cheyenne, Wyoming.

Chapter 15. Two Nevada Robberies

1. Baker, *Wild Bunch at Robbers Roost,* 100–101; Kirby, *Rise and Fall of the Sundance Kid,* 65–66; *Pinkertons,* Sundance Kid file; *SMU,* 94, 100–107.

2. Details are compiled from the *Elko Weekly Independent,* July 15 and 22, 1898; *Elko Free Press,* April 8 and 29, 1899; *Free Press,* September 29, 1900; Donna B. Ernst, "George S. Nixon," 43–48.

3. George S. Nixon Papers; Ernst, "George S. Nixon."

4. *Pinkertons,* Sundance Kid file.

5. *Elko Free Press,* April 8, 1899.

Chapter 16. Wilcox Train Robbery

1. Details are compiled from Athern, *Union Pacific Country;* Union Pacific Railroad Archives, *Carbon County Journal,* June 3, 10, 17 and 24, 1899, and July 3 and 24, 1899; *Buffalo Bulletin,* June 8, 1899; *Natrona County Tribune,* June 8, 1899; *SMU,* pages 108–15; Hadsell's files; Siringo, *Cowboy Detective,* 312–24; Donna B. Ernst, "Wilcox Train Robbery," 34–40; and Mokler, *History of Natrona County,* 320.

2. *Saratoga (Wyo.) Sun,* Saratoga, June 8, 1899.

3. Union Pacific Archives, file # 1655.

4. Ibid.

5. Letter from William Simpson to Charles Kelly, May 5, 1939.

6. Ibid.

7. Mokler, *History of Natrona County*, 318–23.

8. Interviews with Sheperson family; Paul and Donna Ernst, "Wild Bunch Shootout Sites," 50–53.

9. Hadsell's files.

10. In an interview, the Brock family said that some of the jewelry was later given to the museum in Douglas, Wyoming; Ernst, "Wild Bunch Shootout Sites," 50–55.

11. *Carbon County Journal*, June 10, 1899.

12. Brock, *Powder River Country*, 453–56; interview with Brock family.

13. Interview with Brock family.

14. *Carbon County Journal*, June 24, 1899.

15. Letter dated March 6, 1901, from Frank Murray to Frank A. Hadsell, in Hadsell's files.

16. *Pinkertons*, Ryan's dossier.

17. *Rawlins Republican*, June 3 and 8, 1899; *Carbon County Journal*, June 3, 1899.

18. *Pinkertons*, Wilcox "wanted" poster.

19. Copy of deposition, Hadsell's files.

Chapter 17. They Called Her Etta

1. Gillespie, letters.

2. Donna B. Ernst, *Women of the Wild Bunch*, 59–77; Meadows, *Digging Up Butch and Sundance*, 2–8, 11–12, 64, 83, 97; and *Pinkertons*, Etta Place file.

3. *Pinkertons*, Buffalo hospital record in Sundance Kid file.

4. *Pinkertons*, Etta Place file. When the Pinkertons discovered the DeYoung photograph, they also had copies made to circulate throughout the Buffalo, New York, area. The remounted pictures were embossed with the Bliss Brothers of Buffalo logo.

5. *Pinkertons*, Etta Place file.

6. *Pinkertons*, Etta Place file and undated questionnaire from James D. Horan to Frank Dimaio.

7. Local tradition holds that Sundance spent the winter of 1899–1900 on the Little Snake River Valley; the J. D. B. Greig letter suggests he was working for the N Bar N Ranch near Culbertson, Montana, but the evidence is just as strong that he remained in Texas.

Chapter 18. Tipton Train Robbery

1. *Pinkertons*, Sundance Kid file.

2. Early Wild Bunch writers nearly always included Sundance in their list of outlaws at the Tipton train robbery, in part because Sundance had strong ties to Wyoming. In fact, he had originally been expected to participate by his partners in crime. However, the Pinkerton Detective Agency was given evidence to the contrary early in their investigation. Because the Pinkertons kept most of their records private, the early researchers were unable to access their files, and the note explaining Sundance's absence remained hidden for nearly one hundred years. Once the company was sold and their files donated to the Library of Congress, previously unknown pieces of history were suddenly found. The note was one such piece of information. While researchers tended to question how Sundance could have been in Tipton and Winnemucca at nearly the same time, this note found in the Pinkerton files clearly answered the problem. He was not at Tipton. Shortly after its discovery, a British newspaper article about the Winnemucca robbery was uncovered by researcher Mike Bell. The article, a second original source, verified the fact that Sundance was not at Tipton but, instead, was riding the rails on his way to Winnemucca, Nevada.

3. *Pinkertons*, undated Tipton report.

4. Ibid. Sundance Kid file.

5. *Rawlins Republican*, September 5, 1900.

6. Unpublished manuscript by Margaret McIntosh Boice. Interestingly, suspects Jim Ferguson and Bert Charters were married to local girls Rose Lamb and Maude Magor, respectively. Within a few years, three more local girls married men connected with the Wild Bunch—Jano Magor married George Musgrave, Mary Calvert married Elzy Lay, and Louise Hansen married William 'Mike' Dunbar.

7. *Pinkertons*, undated Tipton report.

8. *Rawlins Republican*, December 12, 1900.

9. Ibid., October 22, 1897.

Chapter 19. Three Creek, Idaho

1. All quotes from Sundance's account are from *The Standard*, April 17, 1912, an English newspaper printed in Buenos Aires, Argentina,

and discovered by Wild Bunch researcher Mike Bell. See also, Donna B. Ernst, "Three Creek, Idaho;" *SMU*, 129–45; and the undated booklet *Three Creek History.*

2. *Three Creek History*; the rock store still stands today with the hand-carved initials *J D* and *L D* just to the left side of the doorway.

Chapter 20. Winnemucca Bank Robbery

1. Robbery details are compiled from Paul D. Ernst, "The Winnemucca Bank Holdup," 54–58; Drucker, "Witness Recalls Chasing Robbers"; Button, "Butch Cassidy Gave Getaway Horse to 10-Year Old"; *The Silver State*, September 19, 20, 21, 22, and 27, 1900; Toll, "Butch Cassidy and The Great Winnemucca Bank Robbery," 21–25; Berk, "Who Robbed the Winnemucca Bank?," 11–15; *Elko Free Press*, September 22, 1900; *The Standard*, April 17, 1912; *SMU*, 129–45; and *Pinkertons.*

2. Button, "Butch Cassidy Gave Getaway Horse."

3. Kirby, *Rise and Fall of the Sundance Kid*, 82–87.

4. *Pinkertons*, Informant # 85.

5. Robbery details are compiled from *The Silver State*, September 19, 20, and 27, 1900.

6. Toll, "Butch Cassidy and the Great Winnemucca Bank Robbery"; Horan, *Desperate Men*, 270.

7. Nixon Papers.

8. Button, "Butch Cassidy Gave Getaway Horse."

9. *The Silver State*, September 20, 1900.

10. Letter dated November 28, 1900 to Sheriff Frank Johnson, Nixon Papers.

11. The letters are contained in Nixon Papers.

12. Hadsell's files; William A. 'Mike' Dunbar married Louisa Hansen, who was born in Norway, according to the 1900 Wyoming Federal Census, ED 17. Mike was the younger brother of Jefferson Dunbar, an outlaw who had been killed in Dixon, Wyoming, on July 24, 1898. Mike and Louisa Dunbar reportedly died in Salt Lake City, Utah.

13. Nixon Papers.

14. Letter dated February 21, 1901, Nixon Papers.

15. Letter dated December 9, 1900, to F. Gentsch, Nixon Papers.

16. Ibid.

17. Letter dated August 10, 1902, written in Cholila by Butch to his friend Mrs. Davis, the mother of Maude Davis, who was married to Elzy Lay.

18. Ibid., Meadows, *Digging Up Butch*, xi–xii.
19. Letter dated March 4, 1901, Nixon Papers.
20. Letter to Mr. Fraser, dated February 21, 1901, Nixon Papers.
21. Letter dated March 4, 1901 to Mr. Fraser, Nixon Papers.

Chapter 21. Blackened Gold

1. Hadsell's files; *Pinkertons*, Sundance Kid file.
2. Letter dated February 21, 1901, Nixon Papers.
3. Letter dated December 29, 1900, Hadsell's files.
4. Letter dated December 9, 1900 to F. Gentsch, Nixon Papers.
5. Gooldy memoirs; Gillespie, letters; report by Ayers, *Pinkertons*.
6. Gillespie, letters.
7. Gooldy, memoirs; Gillespie, letters; interviews with Jean Beeler and Ed Wren. That rifle is now housed in the Savery Wyoming Museum.

Chapter 22. Rendezvous in Fort Worth

1. Francis, "End of an Outlaw."
2. Primo Caprera quoted by Dan Buck and Anne Meadows, "Wild Bunch Dream Girl;" Meadows, *Digging Up Butch*, 5; Ernst, *Women of the Wild Bunch*, 65–66.
3. Horan and Sann, *Pictorial History*.
4. Nixons Papers.
5. 1900 Federal Census, Bexar County, Texas, ED 82.
6. *Pinkertons*; "wanted" poster from Malta train robbery—see page 119 in this book.
7. *Pinkertons*, Fanny Porter interview in Sundance Kid file; letter from W. A. P. to J. H. Maddox, dated May 12, 1906.

Chapter 23. Tourists in New York

1. *Pinkertons*, author's interviews with descendants of Samanna Longabaugh Hallman; Sundance's account of the Winnemucca robbery in *The Standard* (April 17, 1912) mentioned a gunshot wound in the arm.
2. *Pinkertons*, undated hospital report.
3. New York City directories, Library of New York City, N.Y.; 1900 Federal Census for New York, ED 320, Sheet 8, lists twenty boarders, including actors and actresses.

4. *Pinkertons*, letter dated July 31, 1902, from Wm. A. Pinkerton to R. A. Pinkerton.

5. Gooldy memoirs; Gillespie, letters. The photograph and letter may have been prompted by the fact that David Gillespie had married Ethel M. Ellis on August 28, 1900, just prior to Sundance's return visit to the Little Snake River Valley during his escape from the Winnemucca bank robbery. The photograph was loaned to a writer in the 1930s and never returned.

6. *Pinkertons*, Criminal History #7111.

7. Dan Buck, e-mail to author, dated November 30, 1999; Letson letter in Charles Kelly's papers.

8. *Pinkertons*, Sundance kid file; New York City directories.

9. Meadows, *Digging Up Butch*, 45.

Chapter 24. Going Straight in Argentina

1. *Pinkertons*, Sundance Kid file; Horan's notes; *SMU*; Meadows, *Digging Up Butch*, 37.

2. Gavirati, "Back at the Ranch."

3. Dan Buck, e-mail to author, dated 22 March 2006.

4. *Pinkertons*, Butch Cassidy file; referenced in Horan's notes.

5. Dan Buck and Anne Meadows, e-mail to author, dated November 30, 1999.

6. *Pinkertons*, Sundance Kid file; *SMU*; *Chicago Tribune*, July 5–7, 1902.

7. "Hotel Touring Club," a tourist booklet used for promotional purposes in 2007, in Trelew, Argentina.

Chapter 25. Mistaken Identity

1. *St. Louis Daily Globe Democrat*, November 6, 1901.

2. Ibid.

3. *San Angelo (Tex.) Standard Times*, November 8, 1901.

Chapter 26. Cholila, Home Sweet Home

1. Meadows, *Digging Up Butch*, xi, quoting Cassidy's 1902 letter to Mrs. Davis.

2. Daniel Buck, "Wild Bunch Cabin Renovation," The Cholila cabin was recently disassembled in a controversial effort to renovate the ranch and turn it into a tourist attraction. A new building was apparently constructed, using some of the old materials.

3. Meadows, *Digging Up Butch*, 5, quoting Primo Capraro.

4. Gavirati, "Frrom the American Far West," 313.

5. Chatwin, *In Patagonia*, 48; Meadows, *Digging Up Butch*, 8; Ernst, *Women of the Wild Bunch*, 65–66.

6. Gavirati, "From the American Far West," 317–18.

7. Meadows, *Digging Up Butch*, xi–xii.

8. Author's interviews of descendants of Samanna Longabaugh Hallman. Samanna kept her diary entries to a minimum, and many of the pages were torn out in an attempt to prevent the Pinkertons from discovering Sundance's whereabouts. Her efforts, however, were for naught since the local postal clerk carefully read her mail and forwarded information to the Philadelphia office of the Pinkertons. (The Philadelphia office was located at 411 Chestnut Street in Philadelphia; and agent Frank P. Dimaio worked there.) Although the diary still exists in a damaged form, all letters were destroyed. An unsigned, wooden souvenir postcard from the St. Louis World's Fair and Exposition was sent to his sister Emma in 1904; the postcard remains in the family today.

9. *Pinkertons*, Dimaio report.

10. *Pinkertons*, cipher list.

11. *Pinkertons*, memo dated March 21, 1909.

12. Dan Buck and Anne Meadows, "Leaving Cholila," Gavirati, From the American West, 317.

13. Meadows, *Digging Up Butch*, 51–57.

14. The post card is still in the family today.

15. *Pinkertons*, Robert A. Pinkerton memo to American Bankers Association, dated October 24, 1904.

16. Buck and Meadows, "Leaving Cholila."

17. *La Prensa* (Buenos Aires), February 16, 1905; *Buenos Aires Herald*, February 16, 1905; Meadows, *Digging Up Butch*.

18. Meadows, *Digging Up Butch*, 67–69; *SMU*, 180.

19. This census provides an unquestionable alibi to the outlaws for the Rio Gallegos bank robbery on February 14, 1905. The bank

holdup, however, brought their presence in Cholila to the attention of the law, and suddenly their peaceful life was over.

Chapter 27. On the Run Again

1. Zuberbuhler, "Butch's Place at Cholila," 36–108, as supplied by Dan Buck.
2. Buck and Meadows, "Leaving Cholila," 21–27.
3. Ibid.
4. *Ozona Kicker,* July 5, 1910; Meadows, *Digging Up Butch,* 10.
5. Horan's notes.
6. Buck and Meadows, "Leaving Cholila," 21–27; Wilson and Evans File.
7. Ibid.
8. Ibid.
9. Daniel Gibbon testified in 1911 that Sundance had told him she remained in San Francisco at least as late as 1906. Coincidentally, Sundance's brother Elwood lived in San Francisco at the time. However, it cannot be proven that she remained in the United States or returned to South America.
10. New York Passenger Lists, Microfilm T715_604, p. 4, lines 24 and 25, in National Archives Records.
11. Completed in July of 1889, the SS *Seguranca* was built in Chester, Pennsylvania, as a 500-plus passenger and cargo vessel. After seeing service during the Spanish-American War, the *Seguranca* was purchased by the Panama Canal Company to provide regular shuttle service for canal workers who traveled frequently between New York City and Colon. If Sundance and Ethel were aboard the ship on this trip, they were among seventeen passengers and crew who came down with yellow fever and were placed in quarantine when they arrived in New York.
12. Horan's notes.

Chapter 28. A Return to Crime

1. *La Nación* (Buenos Aires), December 24, 1905; Meadows, *Digging Up Butch,* 43–45.
2. Dan Buck and Anne Meadows, "Neighbors on the Hot Seat," 6–15.

3. *La Prensa* (Buenos Aires), January 26 and 27, 1906, as translated by Dan Buck.

4. Letter by Roy Letson, in Charles Kelly's papers.

5. Horan's notes.

6. Ibid.

7. Ibid.

8. Ibid.

9. Letter dated November 12, 1907, sent by Butch to the "Boys at Concordia" from Santa Cruz—in Percy Seibert's scrapbook, Robert G. McCubbin Collection.

10. Aller's letter quoted in Meadows, *Digging Up Butch*, 127–28.

11. *New York Herald*, September 23, 1906; *Denver Republican*, September 23, 1906.

12. *Baltimore News*, September 10, 1911.

13. *La Prensa* (Buenos Aires), May 28 and August 25, 1908; *SMU* 180–84.

14. Francis, "End of an Outlaw," 36–43.

Chapter 29. Robbery of the Aramayo Mine Payroll.

1. Robbery details compiled from Meadows, *Digging Up Butch*; Buck and Meadows, "Leaving Cholila"; Buck and Meadows, "Last Days of Butch and Sundance"; and Francis, "End of an Outlaw."

2. Meadows, *Digging Up Butch*, 362–66. Meadows wrote in the Afterword for the 2003 reprint of her book that the local Tupiza newspaper on November 4, 1908, listed Santiago Lowe, a known Cassidy alias, as being registered in the hotel.

3. Meadows, *Digging Up Butch*, 230.

4. Ibid., 228–37.

5. Francis, "End of an Outlaw," 36–43.

Chapter 30. San Vicente, Bolivia

1. Francis, "End of an Outlaw," 36–43.

2. From a letter by Bellot, in Meadows, *Digging Up Butch*, 261.

3. Ibid., 267.

4. All letters and testimony as translated and provided by Meadows, *Digging Up Butch*, 261–62, and 266–68.

5. Ibid., 269–71.

Chapter 31. Who Were Those Guys?

1. Francis, "End of an Outlaw," 36–43.

2. Warner, *Last of the Bandit Riders*, 322.

3. Aller correspondence in Bolivian Foreign Office files for 1910, National Archives Records, Washington, D.C.

4. Meadows, *Digging Up Butch*, 128, quoting Aller's letter dated July 31, 1909.

5. Meadows, 127.

6. Ibid., 129.

Appendix A. Whatever Happened to Ethel?

1. Horan's notes.

2. Meadows, *Digging Up Butch*, 83

Appendix B. Hangers-on and Wanna-bes

1. Letter from Gertrude Phillips to Charles Kelly, October 4, 1938, Kelly's papers.

2. Tanner, *Last of the Old-Time Outlaws*, 70, 190–91, 193.

3. Kirby, *Rise and Fall*, 113.

4. *SMU*, 195–96.

Bibliography

Manuscript and Archival Collections

Boice, Margaret McIntosh. Unpub, memoirs. American Heritage Center, University of Wyoming, Laramie.

Campbell, Charles F. Unpub. collection of livestock history. Montana Historical Society, Helena.

Cornelison, John. "The Wilcox Train Robbery." Unpub. MS. Historical Research Department, Wyoming State Archives, Cheyenne.

Court records. Sundance (Crook County), Wyoming.

Deer Lodge State Prison Records. Montana Historical Society, Helena.

Gillespie, David. Letters and memoirs. Museum of North West Colorado, Craig, Colorado.

Gooldy, John F. Unpub. memoirs. American Heritage Center, University of Wyoming, Laramie.

Hadsell, Sheriff Frank P. Correspondence and papers, #H83-62/28. Wyoming State Archives, Cheyenne.

Horan, James D. Papers, scrapbook, notes from interview with Percy Seibert. Private collection of Robert G. McCubbin, Arizona.

Johnson, Ebb. Unpub. memoirs. Glenbow Institute, Alberta, Calgary, Canada.

Kelly, Charles. Papers and correspondence. Marriott Library, University of Utah, Salt Lake City.

Longabaugh, Harry, Jr. Lecture transcript, June 24, 1970. Weber County Library, Ogden, Utah.

National Archives, Washington, D.C. Census reports, Bolivian Foreign Office files, New York Passenger Lists.

Neidringhaus, A. W. Unpub. collection of livestock history. Montana Historical Society, Helena.

Nixon, George S. Papers and correspondence. Nevada Historical Society. Reno, Nevada.

Pennsylvania Archives. "Associations and Militia."

Pinkerton Detective Agency Archives. Library of Congress. Washington, D.C.

St. Louis, Oliver. Unpub. memoirs. Museum of North West Colorado. Craig, Colorado.

Thomas, John B. Papers of Suffolk Cattle Company. American Heritage Center, University of Wyoming, Laramie,

Union Pacific Railroad Archives. Omaha, Nebraska.

Wilson and Evans File. CENPAT, Puerto Madryn, Argentina. Collection of 1911 depositions by Argentinian authorities into outlaw activities. Supplied and translated by Dan Buck and Anne Meadows.

Books and Articles

Athern, Robert G. *Union Pacific Country.* New York: Rand McNally & Company, 1992.

Baker, Pearl. *The Wild Bunch at Robbers Roost.* New York: Abelard-Schuman, 1971.

Bankston, Wilma Crisp. *Where Eagles Winter: History and Legend of the Disappointment Country.* Cortez, Colo.: Mesa Verde Press, 1988.

Basso, Dave. *Ghosts of Humboldt Region.* Sparks, Nev.: Western Printing & Publishing Co., 1970.

Bean, Theodore W. ed.; *Montgomery County History.* 1884. Norristown, Pa.: Montgomery County Historical Society.

Bell, Mike. "Interview with the Sundance Kid." *WOLA Journal* (Summer 1995).

Berk, Lee. "Who Robbed the Winnemucca Bank?" *Quarterly of the National Association for Outlaw and Lawman History,* (Fall 1983).

Betenson, Lula Parker. *Butch Cassidy, My Brother.* Salt Lake City, Utah: Brigham Young University Press, 1984.

Brand Book of the Montana Stock Growers Association, 1866, 1885. Montana Stock Growers Association. Montana Historical Society, Helena.

Brekke, Alan Lee. *Kid Curry: Train Robber,* Havre, Mont.: Montana, 1989.

Brock, J. Elmer. *Powder River Country.* Cheyenne, Wyo.: Frontier Printing Inc. 1981.

Brown, Mark and W. R. Felton. *Before Barbed Wire.* New York: Bramhall House, 1956.

Buck, Daniel. "Wild Bunch Cabin Renovation Produces Controversy." *WOLA Saddle Bag.* (Summer 2006).

Buck, Dan, and Anne Meadows. "Last Days of Butch and Sundance," *Wild West,* (February 1997).

———, "Leaving Cholila." *True West,* (January 1996).

———, "Neighbors on the Hot Seat." *WOLA Journal,* (Summer 1996).

———, "Wild Bunch Dream Girl." *True West,* (May 2002).

Burroughs, John Rolfe. *Where The Old West Stayed Young.* New York: William Morrow and Company, 1962.

Button, I. Victor. "Butch Cassidy Gave Getaway Horse to 10-Year-Old." *Newsletter of the National Association for Outlaw and Lawman History* (Spring 1974).

Chapman, Arthur. "Butch Cassidy." *The Elks Magazine.* (April 1930).

Chatwin, Bruce. *In Patagonia.* New York: Penguin Books, 1977.

Churchill, E. Richard. *They Rode with Butch Cassidy, The McCartys.* Gunnison, Colo.: B & B Printers, 1972.

DeJournette, Dick and Daun; *One Hundred Years of Brown's Park and Diamond Mountain.* Bernal, Utah: DeJournette Enterprises, 1996.

Drucker, Edward A. "Witness Recalls Chasing Robbers." *Humboldt Sun,* September 16, 1982.

Dullenty, Jim. "The Strange Case of Sundance Kid Junior." *Newsletter of the National Association for Outlaw and Lawman History.* (Winter 1991).

Engebretson, Doug. *Empty Saddles, Forgotten Names.* Aberdeen, S.D.: North Plains Press, 1984.

Ernst, Donna B. "The Butte County Bank Holdup" *Old West* (Fall 1997).

———. "A Deadwood Jail Break," *True West* (January 2000).

———. "Friends of the Pinkertons," *NOLA Quarterly* (April-June 1995).

———. "George S. Nixon," *WOLA Journal* (Summer 2001).

———. "The Snake River Valley and the Sundance Kid." *Frontier Magazine* (August 1997).

———. "Sundance, The Missing Years," *Old West* (Spring 1994).

———. *Sundance, My Uncle.* College Station, Tex.: Early West, 1992.

———. "Three Creek Idaho." *Wild West* (December 2001).

———. "Walt Punteney and Tom O'Day." *Wild West* (April 2004).

————. "The Wilcox Train Robbery." *Wild West* (June 1999).

————. *Women of the Wild Bunch.* Kearney, Nebr.: Wild Bunch Press, 2004.

————. "Wyoming Cowboy." *WOLA Journal* (Spring 1992).

Ernst, Paul, and Donna Ernst. "Wild Bunch Shootout Sites." *WOLA Journal* (Fall 1999).

Ernst, Paul D. "The Winnemucca Bank Holdup." *Wild West* (June 1998).

Francis, A. G. "The End of an Outlaw." *Wide World* (May 1913).

French, Captain William. *Recollections of a Western Ranchman.* 1928. Silver City, N.M. High-Lonesome Books, reprint 1990.

From Buffalo Bones to Sonic Boom. Glasgow, Mont.: Glasgow Jubilee Committee, 1962.

Garman, Mary. "Harry Longabaugh—The Sundance Kid, The Early Years, 1867–1889." *Bits and Pieces* Vol II no. 3 (Newcastle, Wyo. 1977).

Gatchell, Thelma. "Hole in the Wall." *Annals of Wyoming,* 1958.

Gavirati, Marcelo. "Back at the Ranch." *True West* (December 2002).

————. "From the American Far West to the Argentine Far South." *Patagonia: 13,000 Years of History.* Buenos Aires: Museo Lelegue 2001.

History of Nevada. Oakland, Calif.: Thomas Thompson and Albert West, 1881. Rept.: Reno: Howell-North, 1958.

Horan, James D. *Desperate Men.* New York: G. P. Putnam's Sons, 1949.

————. *The Outlaws,* New York: Crown Publishing Inc., 1977.

————, and Paul Sann. New York: *Pictorial History of the Wild West.* Crown Publishing Inc., 1954.

Ings, Fred. *Before the Fences.* Calgary, Canada: McAra Printing, Ltd., 1980.

Jessen, Kenneth. *Colorado Gunsmoke.* Boulder, Colo.: Pruett Pub. 1986.

Kelly, Charles. *The Outlaw Trail, The Story of Butch Cassidy and The Wild Bunch.* New York: Bonanza Books, 1959.

Kirby, Edward M. *The Rise & Fall of the Sundance Kid.* Iola, Wisc.: Western Publications, 1983.

Kouris, Diana Allen. *The Romantic and Notorious History of Brown's Park.* Greybull, Wyo.: The Wolverine Gallery, 1988.

Leaves from the Medicine Tree, High River Pioneers and Old Timers Association, Lethbridge, Alberta, 1960.

Mather, Sam W. *Frontier Times* (October 1928).

McCarty, Tom. *Tom McCarty's Own Story, Autobiography of an Outlaw.* Hamilton, Mont.: Rocky Mt. House, 1986.

McCoy, Tim, and Ronald McCoy. *Tim McCoy Remembers the West,* New York Doubleday: 1977.

McLoughlin, Denis. *The Wild and Woolly, An Encyclopedia of the Old West,* New York: Doubleday, 1975.

Meadows, Anne. *Digging Up Butch and Sundance.* New York: St. Martin's Press, 1994.

Menefee, George W.; *Cow Talk,* memoirs as recorded by Lottie W. Reddert. Cortez, Colo.

Mokler, Alfred James. *The History of Natrona County, Wyoming, 1888–1922.* New York: R. R. Donnelley & Sons Company, 1923.

Morgan, Dale L. *The Humboldt, Highroad of the West.* Humboldt, Nev.: J. J. Little and Ives Co., 1943.

Neidringhaus, Lee I. *The N Bar N Ranch,* New York, 2004.

Paher, Stanley W. *Nevada Ghost Towns & Mining Camps.* Reno: Howell-North Books, 1970.

―――. *Nevada Towns & Tales, Vol. I–North.* Reno: Nevada Publications 1981.

Patterson, Richard. *Butch Cassidy, A Biography.* Bison rept. Lincoln: University of Nebraska Press, 1998.

―――. *Historical Atlas of the Outlaw West.* Boulder, Colo.: Johnson Books, 1985.

Pennypacker, Samuel Whitaker, Esq., *Annals of Phoenixville and Its Vicinity: From Settlement to the Year 1871.* Philadelphia: Bavis & Pennypacker, 1872.

Piernes, Justin. "Butch Cassidy en la Patagonia." *Clarin,* May 2, 3, and 4, 1970.

Pointer, Larry. *In Search of Butch Cassidy.* Norman: University of Oklahoma, 1977.

Rupp, Prof. I. Daniel. *Immigrants in Pennsylvania.*

Segars, Loretta, *100 Years in Culbertson.* Culbertson, Mont.: Culbertson Centennial Steering Committee, 1986.

Selcer, Richard F. *Hell's Half Acre,* Fort Worth, Tex.: Texas Christian University Press, 1991.

Sheppard, Bert. "Just About Nothing." Calgary, Alberta: Glenbow Institute.

Siringo, Charles A. *A Cowboy Detective.* Rept., Lincoln: University of Nebraska Press, 1988.

Swallow, Alan, ed. *The Wild Bunch.* Denver: Sage Books, 1966.

Tanner, Karen Holliday, and John D. Tanner, Jr. *Last of the Old-Time Outlaws.* Norman: University of Oklahoma, 2002.

Tennent, William L. *John Jarvie of Brown's Park, Utah.* Vernal, Utah: Bureau of Land Management, 1982.

Three Creek History. Twin Falls: Historical Society of Owyhee County, Idaho.

Toll, David W. "Butch Cassidy & The Great Winnemucca Bank Robbery." *Nevada* (May-June 1983).

Van Dersal & Connor. *Stockgrowers' Directory of Marks and Brands*, Helena, Mont.: Van Dersal & Connor.

Warner, Matt. *The Last of the Bandit Riders*. New York: Bonanza Books, 1950.

Willis, Ann Bassett. "Queen Ann." *Colorado Magazine* (April 1952).

Zuberbuhler, Luisa. "Butch's Place at Cholila." *Lugares Magazine* no. 10, 1992.

Index

227